Statistical Methods
for Practice and Research

Statistical Methods
for Practice and Research

A guide to data analysis using SPSS

Ajai S. Gaur
Sanjaya S. Gaur

Response Books
A division of SAGE Publications
New Delhi ♦ Thousand Oaks ♦ London

First published in 2006 by

Response Books
A division of Sage Publications India Pvt Ltd
B1/I 1, Mohan Cooperative Industrial Area
Mathura Road
New Delhi 110 044
www.sagepub.in

Sage Publications Inc	**Sage Publications Ltd**
2455 Teller Road	1 Oliver's Yard
Thousand Oaks	55 City Road,
California 91320	London EC1Y 1SP

Published by Tejeshwar Singh for Response Books, typeset in 11/13.5 Palatino by Star Compugraphics Private Limited, Delhi and printed at Chaman Enterprises, New Delhi.

Fifth Printing 2008

Library of Congress Cataloging-in-Publication Data

Gaur, Ajai S., 1977–
    Statistical methods for practice and research: a guide to data analysis
  using SPSS/Ajai S. Gaur, Sanjaya S. Gaur.
        p. cm.
    Includes bibliographical references.
    1. SPSS (Computer file)   2. Social sciences—Statistical methods—Computer programs.   3. Social sciences—Research—Statistical methods.
    I. Gaur, Sanjaya S., 1969–   II. Title.

HA32.G38	005.5'5—dc22	2006	2006015343

ISBN: 10: 0-7619-3502-9 (PB)   10: 81-7829-657-8 (India-PB)
        13: 978-0-7619-3502-5 (PB)   13: 978-81-7829-657-9 (India-PB)

Sage Production Team: Anindita Pandey, Girish Sharma and Santosh Rawat

To our parents

Shri Ram Saran and Smt. Sumitra

Contents

Preface

For business managers and practicing researchers, many times it becomes difficult to solve the real life problems involving statistical methods using software packages. The books on managerial statistics do give a comprehensive picture of statistics as a facilitating tool for managerial decision-making but they invariably fail in helping the manager/researcher in solving and getting results for practical problems. With the help of simple examples, these books very successfully explain simple calculation procedures as well as the concepts behind them. However manual calculations, being cumbersome, tiresome and error-prone can be successful only to the extent of explaining the concepts and not for solving the real life research problems involving huge amount of data.

For this reason, most of the practical statistical analyses is done with the help of an appropriate software package. A manager/researcher, is only required to prepare the input data and should be able to get the final result easily with the help of software packages, so that focused attention can be given to various other aspects of problem solving and decision making.

A wide variety of software packages such as SPSS, Minitab, SAS, STATA, S-PLUS etc. are available for statistical analyses. Microsoft Excel can also be used very successfully to solve a wide variety of problems. Some books on managerial statistics even provide with spreadsheet templates where different results can be obtained by changing the input data. However, without the practical knowledge of working with a specialized software package, such templates are not helpful beyond academic interest.

This book is an effort towards facilitating business managers and researchers in solving statistical problems using computers. We have chosen SPSS, which is a very comprehensive and widely available package for statistical analyses. We have illustrated its usage with the help of simple practical problems. The objective is to make the readers understand how they can use various statistical techniques for their own research problems. Throughout the book, point and click method has been used in place of writing the syntax, even though syntax has been provided for interested users at the end of each analysis. The advantage of the point and click method is that it does not require any advance knowledge of the syntax and altogether eliminates the need to learn different types of command for different analyses.

The book is aimed primarily at academic researchers, MBA students, doctoral, masters and undergraduate students of mathematics, management science and various other science and social science disciplines, practicing managers, marketing research professionals etc. It is also expected to serve as a companion volume to any standard text book of Statistics and Marketing Research and for use in such courses in business schools and engineering colleges.

The book comprises of 11 chapters. Chapter 1 presents a brief overview of SPSS. Chapter 2 gives an overview of basic statistical concepts with the aim of helping in a quick revision of basic concepts, which one commonly encounters while carrying out data analyses. For an in-depth understanding of these concepts, readers are advised to refer to any standard text book on statistics. Chapter 3 presents the use of SPSS in calculating descriptive statistics and presenting a visual display of the data. Chapters 4 and 5 present statistical techniques for comparing means of two or more than two groups. Chapter 6 describes a chi-square test for discrete data. Correlation analyses is presented in Chapter 7, followed by multiple regression in Chapter 8 and logistic regression in Chapter 9. Finally, we present data reduction techniques and methods for establishing scale reliability in Chapter 10 and advanced data handling and manipulation techniques in Chapter 11.

The illustrations are based on the SPSS 14.0 version. However, earlier versions of SPSS (10, 11, 12, 13) are functionally not much different from this version. The users of the earlier versions will find it equally useful for their purpose. With this book, we hope, you can analyze your data on your own, and appreciate the real use of statistics.

Acknowledgements

Many people have made this book possible. We would especially like to thank our students and participants of the research methods workshops we conducted all over India for refining our thinking and for motivating us to write a text on this subject. Our sincere thanks are due to Andrew Delios for his unusual tutelage on finer aspects of data analyses. The publishing team at Sage, New Delhi has been very helpful. Leela, Shweta and Anindita need special mention for their patience and support during the publication process. We would also like to thank Chapal, without whose persistence this book would have never come out. Finally, we thank our families—Sanjaya's family: Nirmal, Kamaksi and Vikrant, and Ajai's family: Deeksha—for their continued support and encouragement, without which this project would not have been attempted, much less finished.

Ajai S. Gaur
Sanjaya S. Gaur

1

Introduction to SPSS

SPSS is a very powerful and user friendly program for statistical analyses. Anyone with a basic knowledge of statistics who is familiar with *Microsoft Office* can easily learn how to run very complicated analyses in SPSS with a simple click of the mouse. We begin this chapter from how to open the SPSS program and go on to explain different menus on the tool bar, the starting commands, and the basic procedures of data entry.

1.1 STARTING SPSS

The SPSS program can be installed in a computer using a CD or from the network. A free trial version of the program can be obtained using the coupon provided at the end of this book. Once installed, SPSS can be opened like any other Windows-based application by clicking on the *Start* menu at the bottom left hand corner of the screen and clicking on *SPSS for Windows* from the list of programs. Opening the SPSS program for the first time will produce a dialogue box as shown in Figure 1.1. This dialogue box is not of any particular use, select *Don't show this dialogue box in the future*, and click on the *Cancel* button. This activates a window as shown in Figure 1.2. This is the main data editor window where all the data is entered, much like an Excel spreadsheet. A quick look at this screen (Figure 1.2) reveals that it is quite similar to most of the other Windows-based applications such as MS Excel.

At the top of the screen there are different menus, which give access to various functions of SPSS. Below this, there is a toolbar, which has buttons for quick access to various functions. The same functions can be performed by choosing relevant options from the menus. At the bottom of the screen we have a status bar. At the bottom of Figure 1.2, we can see *"SPSS Processor is ready"* in the status bar. It implies that SPSS has been installed properly and the license is valid. If the analysis is being run by the processor, status bar shows a message to that effect. The program can be closed by clicking on the close button at the top right hand corner, just like in any other Windows application software.

1.2 SPSS MAIN MENUS

SPSS 14.0 has 11 main menus, which provide access to every tool of the SPSS program. You can see the menus on the top of Figure 1.2. Readers must be familiar with some of the menu items like *File, Edit* etc. as these are

Figure 1.1

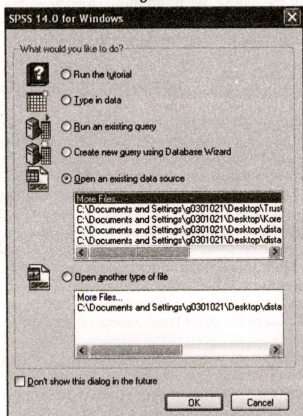

Figure 1.2

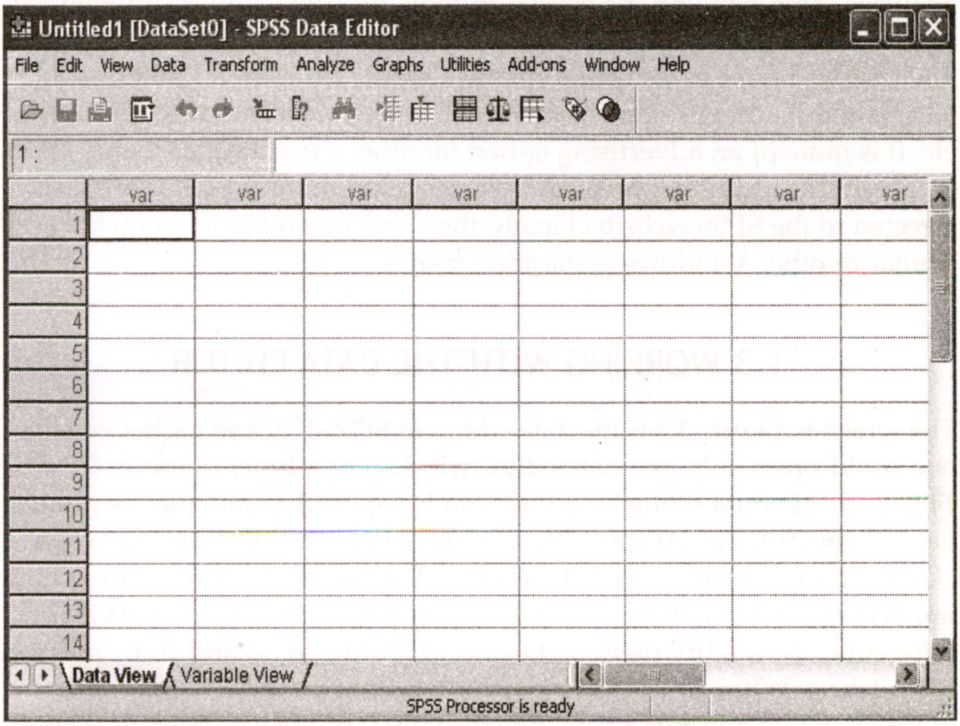

commonly encountered while working on *Microsoft Office* applications. We will go through the menus in this section.

The *File*, *Edit* and *View* menus are very similar to what we get on opening a spreadsheet. The *File* menu lets us open, save, print and close files and provides access to recently used files. The *Edit* menu lets us do things like cut, copy, paste etc. The *View* menu lets us customize the SPSS desktop. Using the *View* menu we can hide or show the toolbar, status bar, gridlines etc.

The *Data* menu is an important tool in SPSS. It allows us to manipulate the data in various ways. We can define variables, go to a particular case, sort cases, transpose them, merge cases as well as variables from some other file. We can also select cases on which we want to run the analysis and split the file to arrange the output of analysis in a particular manner. The *Transform* menu is another very useful tool, which lets us compute new variables and make changes to existing ones.

The *Analyze* menu is the function which lets us perform all the statistical analyses. This has various statistical tools grouped under different categories. The *Graph* menu lets us make various types of plots from our data. The *Utilities* menu gives us information about variables and files. *Add-ons* tells us about other programs of the SPSS family such as Amos, Clementine etc. It is more of an advertising option for other programs, as it only briefs us about the additional programs. For detailed information, the users are directed to the SPSS website. Finally, the *Windows* and *Help* menu are very similar to other Windows application menus.

1.3 WORKING WITH THE DATA EDITOR

The screen in Figure 1.2 is the data editor. In SPSS 13.0 and earlier versions, one could open only one data editor window at a time, however in SPSS 14.0, multiple data editor windows can be opened simultaneously, much like Microsoft Excel. At the bottom of the data editor there are two tabs— *Data View* and *Variable View*. When in *Data View*, the data editor works pretty much in the same manner as an Excel spreadsheet. One can enter values in different cells, modify them and even cut and paste to and from an Excel spreadsheet. When in *Variable View*, the data editor window looks as shown in Figure 1.3. In addition to entering the values of the variables, we have to provide information about them in SPSS. This can be done when the data editor is in *Variable View*. Notice that there are 10 columns in the data editor window in Figure 1.3. We will explain the usage of each of them with the help of following small exercise of data entry:

Suppose we want to enter the following data in SPSS:

Respondent	Gender (M=1, F=2)	Age
1	1	25
2	1	22
3	2	20
4	2	27
5	2	28

Figure 1.3

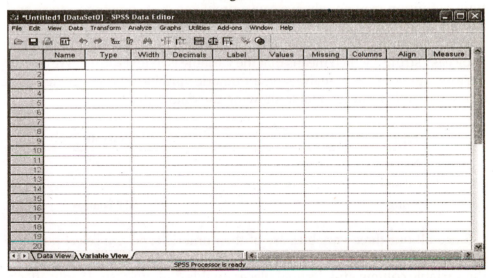

We have three variables to enter—respondent number, gender and age. The first column in the variable view is *Name.* Earlier versions of SPSS (SPSS 12.0 and earlier) could take a maximum of eight characters starting with a letter to identify a variable. There is no limit for the length of variable name in SPSS 13.0 and SPSS 14.0. In this example, we will name respondent number as resp_id; gender and age can be named as they are. The next column titled *Type* lets us define the variable type. If we click on the cell next to variable name and in the *Type* column, we get a dialogue box as shown in Figure 1.4.

Figure 1.4

Data can be of several types, including numeric, date, text etc. An incorrect type-definition may not always cause problems, but sometimes does, and should therefore be avoided. The most common type used is "numeric," which means that the variable has a numeric value. The other common choice is "string," which means that the variable is in text format. We cannot perform any statistical analysis on a numeric variable if it is specified as a string variable. Below is a table showing the data types:

Type	Example
Numeric	1,000.01
Comma	1,000.01
String	IIT Bombay

Since all our three variables are of the numeric type, we select numeric from the dialogue box shown in Figure 1.4. We can also specify the width of the variable column and decimal places on this dialogue box. It only affects the way variables are shown when the data editor is on data view. Click on *OK* to return to the data editor. Next two columns titled *Width* and *Decimals* also allow us to specify these factors for the data view. Please note that these have no impact on the actual values we enter in the data editor, they only affect the display of the data. For example if the value of a variable in a particular cell is 100000000, which comprises of 9 digits and we have specified the width for this variable as 8, it will appear as ########. This simply means that the width of the variable column is not enough to display the variable correctly.

Next, we have a column titled *Label*. Since the variable name in the first column can only be of 8 characters in the earlier versions of the SPSS program, it is sometimes difficult to identify the variable by its name. To avoid this problem, we can write the details about a particular variable in this column. For example, we can write "Respondent identification number" as label for *resp_id* variable. We can ask the SPSS program to show variable labels with or without the names in the output window. This option can be activated by selecting "Names" and "Labels" from the dialogue box obtained by clicking Edit → Options → Output Labels.

Then, we have a column labeled *Values.* If we click on the cell next to the variable name and in the *Values* column, we get a dialogue box as shown in Figure 1.5. In this box, we can specify values for our variables. In the example

Figure 1.5

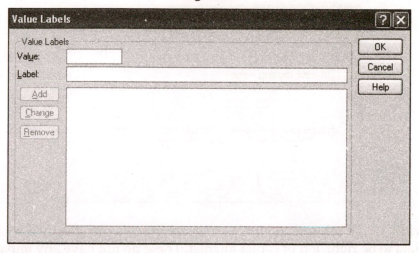

here, we have two values for gender—1 representing male and 2 representing female. Enter 1 in the empty box labeled *Value* and specify its name (Male) in the next box labeled *Value Label*. This will activate the *Add* button. Click on this button and repeat these steps to specify female. This way we can keep track of the actual status of qualitative variables such as gender, nation, race, color etc.

After *values* we have a column labeled *Missing* to specify missing values. While coding data, we often specify certain numbers to variables for which some respondents have given no response. Unless we specify these values as missing values, SPSS will take them into consideration for data analyses producing a wrong output. One way to handle this problem is to recode these numbers to missing values. The *Recode* command has been discussed in section 11.6. The other way is to specify the number that should be considered as missing values here itself. Clicking on the cell next to the variable name and in the *Missing* column will produce a dialogue box as shown in Figure 1.6. By default, *No missing values* is selected here. We can specify up to 3 discrete values to be considered as missing values. Alternatively, specify a range and all the values in the range will be considered as missing values. In case there are more than 3 discrete values that cannot be specified as a range, use the *Recode* command from the *Transform* menu.

The next two columns titled *Columns* and *Align* help us modify the way we want to view the data on screen. In the *Columns* column we can specify

Figure 1.6

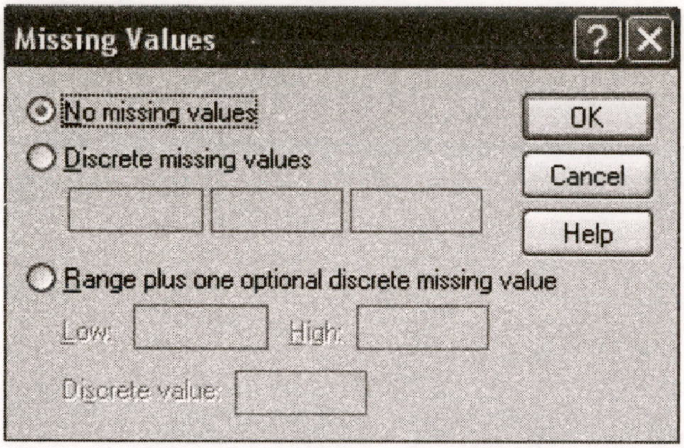

the width of the column and in the *Align* column we can specify if we want our data to be right, left or center aligned. These do not have any impact on the actual data analyses. Finally, in the column titled *Measure*, we can specify whether our variable is scale, ordinal or nominal. SPSS treats interval and ratio data as scale. Different categories of variables are explained in Chapter 2.

Once the variables are specified, you can switch to *Data View* and enter the data. The data editor on entering the data will look as shown in Figure 1.7. This data file can be saved just as an MS Word or MS Excel file and reopened by double clicking on the file from its saved location.

1.4 SPSS VIEWER

Whenever we run any command in SPSS, the output is shown in the SPSS Viewer which opens as a separate window. We can also specify the commands to be displayed in log in the Viewer window. This option can be activated by selecting *Display commands in log* option on the dialogue box, obtained by clicking Edit → Options → Viewer. If this option is selected, a Viewer window will open displaying the save command once we save the file. The Viewer window is shown in Figure 1.8.

The SPSS Viewer window has two panels. The right hand panel shows the actual output and log of commands (if the same is activated), the left hand panel shows an outline of the output shown in the right hand panel. One can quickly navigate through the output by selecting the same from the outline provided in the left hand panel.

Figure 1.7

Figure 1.8

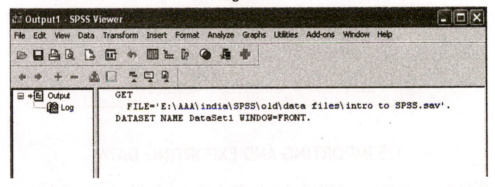

The menu items are quite similar to what we find on the Data Editor. However, here we have two additional menus—*Insert* and *Format.* The *Insert* command can be used to insert headings, comments, page breaks etc. to organize the output if the output file is very large. The *Format* command has a similar role of arranging the output in a user friendly manner. The *Format* command is rarely used as the output can be copied and pasted onto a MS Word or MS Excel file. The output can also be exported to a variety of other formats. The export option can be accessed under the *File* menu. Clicking on *Export* will produce a dialogue box as shown in Figure 1.9. On this window we can specify the part of the output we want to export from the drop down menu against *Export.* We can also specify the format of the exported file by selecting a particular file type from the drop down menu below *File Type.* SPSS provides four formats in which the output can be exported—HTML file, Text file, Excel file, and Word/RTF file.

Figure 1.9

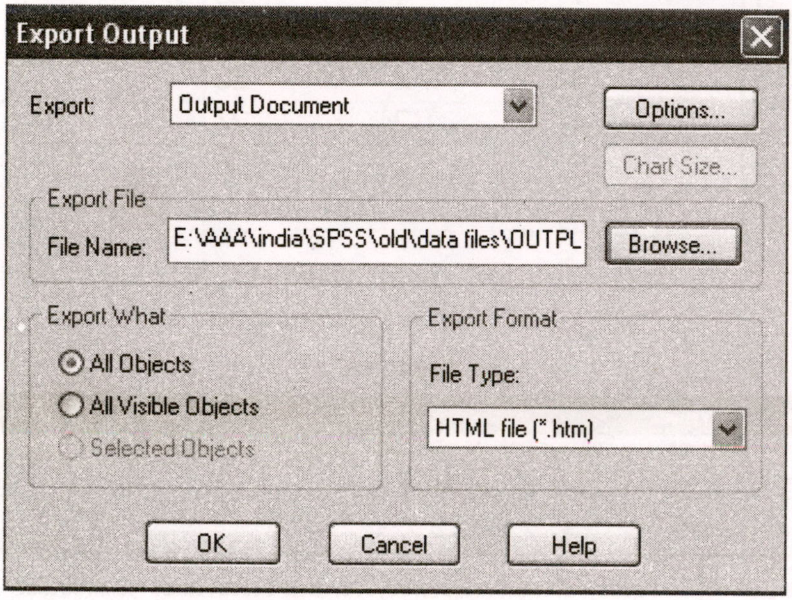

1.5 IMPORTING AND EXPORTING DATA

SPSS gives users a variety of options to open a data file. Click on File → Open → Data... as shown in Figure 1.10. This will produce a dialogue box (Figure 1.11).

Here we can choose the types of file we want to open in SPSS. The file type can be chosen from the drop down menu against *Files of Type* as shown in Figure 1.11. SPSS 14.0 can open data files from programs like Excel, Systat,

Figure 1.10

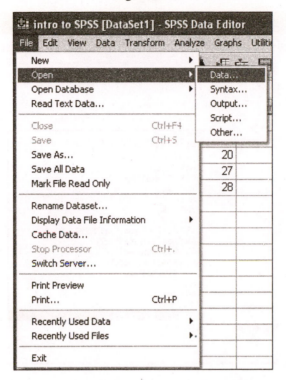

Lotus, dBase, SAS, STATA in addition to text and ASCII formats. SPSS 14.0 is an improvement as it can support more file types such as STATA files, which was not possible in earlier versions.

If we want to open data from an Excel file, we select the file and click on *Open.* This will produce a dialogue box as shown in Figure 1.12. In this dialogue box, we can specify the specific work sheet from which we want to import the data. We can also read the variable names if the same have been specified in the Excel sheet by clicking on a small box against *Read variable names from the first row of data.* Please note that if the variable names specified in Excel have more than eight characters, SPSS 12.0 and earlier versions would assign a name to them automatically as they do not support variable names bigger than eight characters.

Figure 1.11

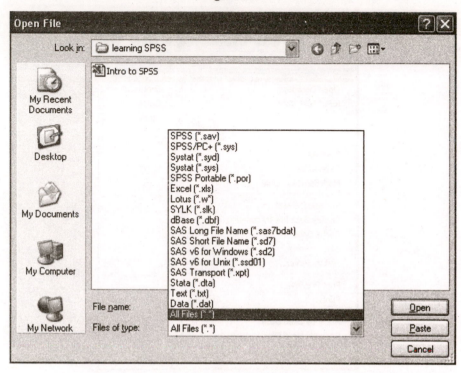

Figure 1.12

Just as we can import data into SPSS from many formats, we can also save a SPSS data file into different formats. This can be done by clicking on *File Save as* and selecting the required format in the resulting dialogue box.

2

Basic Statistical Concepts

Computers have changed the way statistics is learned and taught. Often, students of behavioral sciences are interested only in the 'results' of their 'analyses' and do not care about how the results are obtained. The purpose of this chapter is to introduce such readers to the common statistical terms and concepts which one must know in order to interpret computer generated outputs. This is not to under-emphasize the value of learning the nitty-gritty of statistical techniques. Readers are strongly recommended to refer to some standard statistical text book in order to understand the underlying theory and logic. However, as the objective of this book is to help students use SPSS for their research, we limit the discussion in this chapter to the practical aspects of statistics necessary for using a software package, capable of doing statistical analyses for us.

2.1 RESEARCH IN BEHAVIORAL SCIENCES

One of the main objectives of a behavioral scientist is to develop theories and principles which provide insights into human and organizational behavior. These theories and principles have to be evaluated against actual observations. This is called the validation of theories by empirical research. Broadly, research can be classified into two groups—qualitative research and quantitative research.

2.1.1 Qualitative Research

Qualitative research involves collecting qualitative data by way of in-depth interviews, observations, field notes, open-ended questions etc. The researcher himself is the primary data collection instrument, and the data could be collected in the form of words, images, patterns etc. Data analysis involves searching for patterns, themes and holistic features. Results of such research are likely to be context specific and reporting takes the form of a narrative with contextual description and direct quotations from researchers.

2.1.2 Quantitative Research

Quantitative research involves collecting quantitative data based on precise measurement using structured, reliable and validated data collection instruments or through archival data sources. The nature of the data is in the form of variables and data analysis involves establishing statistical relationships. If properly done, results of such research are generalizable to entire populations. Without any specific prejudice against these two research approaches, the rest of the book deals only with quantitative research.

Quantitative research could be classified into two groups depending on the data collection methodologies—experimental research, and non-experimental research. The choice of statistical analysis depends on the nature of the research.

Experimental Research forms the basis of much of the psychological research. The main purpose of experimental research is to establish a cause and effect relationship. Please note that it is only in a properly designed experimental research that a researcher can establish a cause and effect relationship conclusively. The defining characteristics of experimental research are active manipulation of independent variables and the random assignment of participants to the conditions which represent these variations. Other than the independent variables to be manipulated, everything else should be kept as similar and as constant as possible.

To depict the way experiments are conducted, we use a term called design of experiment. There are two main types of experimental designs—between-subjects design, and within-subjects design. In a between-subjects design, we randomly assign different participants to different conditions. On the other hand, in a within-subjects design the same participants are randomly allocated to more than one condition. It is also referred to as repeated measures design. In addition to having a purely between-subjects or within-subjects design, one can also have a mixed design experiment. The commonly used techniques for analyzing such data include *t*-tests, ANOVA etc.

Non-Experimental Research is commonly used in sociology, political science and management disciplines. This kind of research is often done with the help of a survey. There is no random assignment of participants to a particular group, nor do we manipulate the independent variables. As a result, one can not establish a cause and effect relationship through non-experimental research. There are two approaches to analyzing such data. First is testing for significant differences across the groups (such as IQ levels of participants from different ethnic backgrounds), while the second is testing for significant association between two factors (such as firm sales and advertising expenditure).

Quantitative research is also classified based on the type of data used as primary and secondary data research. Primary data is the one which we collect directly from the subjects of study. This is done with the help of standard survey instrument. An example of this kind of research will be a 360-degree performance evaluation of employees in organizations. Secondary data (also known as archival data) on the other hand is collected from published sources. There are many database management firms, which keep a record of different kinds of micro- and macro-environmental data. For example, the United States Patent and Trademarks Office (USPTO, www.uspto.gov) has detailed information about all the patents filed in the United States. Some other commonly used sources of secondary data include company reports, trade journals and magazines, newspaper clippings etc. Many times, the secondary data is supplemented by data collected from primary methods such as surveys.

2.2 TYPES OF VARIABLES

A variable is a characteristic of an individual or object that can be measured. There are two types of variables—qualitative and quantitative.

2.2.1 Qualitative Variables

Qualitative variables are those variables which differ in kind rather than degree. These could be measured on nominal or ordinal scales.

(i)　The **nominal scale** indicates categorizing into groups or classes. For example, gender, religion, race, color, occupation etc.

(ii) The **ordinal scale** indicates ordering of items. For example, agreement-disagreement scale (1—strongly agree to 5—strongly disagree), consumer satisfaction ratings (1—totally satisfied to 5—totally dissatisfied) etc.

Qualitative data could be dichotomous in which there are only two categories (for example, gender) or multinomial in which there are more than two categories (for example, geographic region).

2.2.2 Quantitative Variables

Quantitative variables are those variables which differ in degree rather than kind. These could be measured on interval or ratio scales.

(i) The **interval scale** indicates rank and distance from an arbitrary zero measured in unit intervals. For example, temperature, examination scores etc.

(ii) The **ratio scale** indicates rank and distance from a natural zero. For example, height, monthly consumption, annual budget etc.

SPSS does not differentiate between interval and ratio data and lists them under the label *Scale*.

2.3 RELIABILITY AND VALIDITY

Reliability and validity are two important characteristics of any measurement procedure. Reliability refers to the confidence we can place on the measuring instrument to give us the same numeric value when the measurement is repeated on the same object. Validity on the other hand means that our measuring instrument actually measures the property it is supposed to measure. Reliability of an instrument does not warranty its validity.

For example, there may be an instrument which can measure the number of things a child can recall from his last one day's activities. If this instrument returns the same value when implemented on the same child, it is a reliable instrument. But if someone claims that it is a valid instrument for measuring the IQ level of the child, he may be wrong. This instrument may just be measuring the memory level and not the IQ level of the child.

2.3.1 Assessing Reliability

As discussed earlier, reliability is the degree to which one may expect to find the same result if a measurement is repeated. One way to ideally measure reliability is by the test-retest method. It is done by measuring the same object twice and correlating the results. If the measurement generates the same answer in repeated attempts, it is reliable. However, establishing reliability through test-retest is practically very difficult. Once a subject has been put through some test, it will no longer remain neutral to the test. Imagine taking the same GMAT test repeatedly to establish the reliability of the test!

Some of the commonly used techniques for assessing reliability include Cohen's *kappa coefficient* for categorical data and Cronbach's *alpha* for internal reliability of a set of questions (scales). Advanced tests of reliability can be performed using confirmatory factor analysis.

2.3.2 Assessing Validity

The objective of assessing validity is to see how accurate is the relationship between the measure and the underlying trait it is trying to measure. The first step in assessing validity is called the **face validity test**. Face validity establishes whether the measuring device looks like it is measuring the correct characteristics. The face validity test is done by showing the instrument to experts and actual subjects and analyzing their responses qualitatively. Experts, however, do not give much importance to face validity. Three other important aspects of validity are predictive validity, content validity, and construct validity.

Predictive validity means that the measurement should be able to predict other measures of the same thing. For example, if a student is doing well on the GMAT examination, she should also do well during her MBA program.

Content Validity refers to the extent to which a measurement reflects the specific intended domain of content. For example, if a researcher wants to assess the English language skills of students and develops a measurement which tests for how well the students can read; such a measurement clearly lacks content validity. English language skills include many other things besides reading (writing, listening, etc.). Reading does not reflect the entire domain of behaviors which characterize English language skills. To establish content validity, researchers should first define the entire domain of their study and then assess if the instrument they are using truly represents this domain.

Construct validity is one of the most commonly used techniques in social sciences. Based on theory, it looks for expected patterns of relationships among variables. Construct validity thus tries to establish an agreement between the measuring instrument and theoretical concepts. To establish construct validity, one must first establish a theoretical relationship and examine the empirical relationships. Empirical findings should then be interpreted in terms of how they clarify the construct validity.

2.4 HYPOTHESIS TESTING

A hypothesis is an assumption or claim about some characteristic of a population, which we should be able to support or reject on the basis of empirical evidence. For example, an electric bulb manufacturing company may claim that the average life of its bulbs is at least 1000 hours.

Hypothesis testing is a process for choosing between different alternatives. The alternatives have to be mutually exclusive and exhaustive. Being mutually exclusive means when one is true the other is false and vice-versa. Being exhaustive means that there should not be any possibility of any other relationship between the parameters. In the example of the electric bulb manufacturer, the following two options will have to be considered to verify the manufacturer's claim:

1. Average life of the bulb is greater than or equal to 1000 hours.
2. Average life of the bulb is less than 1000 hours.

We can see that these options are mutually exclusive as well as exhaustive. Typically, in hypothesis testing, we have two options to choose from. These are termed as null hypothesis and alternate hypothesis.

Null Hypothesis (H_0)—It is the presumption that is accepted as correct unless there is strong evidence against it.

Alternative Hypothesis (H_1)—It is accepted when H_0 is rejected.

Null hypothesis represents the status quo and alternate hypothesis is the negation of the status-quo situation. Proper care should be taken while formulating null and alternate hypotheses. One way to ensure that null hypothesis is formulated correctly is to observe that when null hypothesis is accepted, no corrective action is needed.

In the electric bulb example, the first option that the average life of the bulb is greater than or equal to 1000 hours is the null hypothesis. Negation of this claim would mean acceptance of the second option that the average life of the bulb is less than 1000 hours. This is the alternate hypothesis for the given example. Readers may note that negation of the null hypothesis also means that some corrective action is needed to ensure that the average life of bulbs is at least 1000 hours.

Hypothesis testing helps in decision-making in real life business, economics and research-related problems. Some of the examples are:

- *Marketing:* The marketing department wants to know if a particular marketing campaign had any impact in increasing the level of product awareness.
- *Production:* The production department wants to know if the average output from two factories is the same.
- *Finance:* The finance department wants to know if the average stock price of the company's stocks has been less than that of the competitor's stocks.
- *Human Resource:* The HR department wants to know if there has been any significant impact of the 360-degree feedback system on employees' performance.
- *Quality Control:* The quality control department wants to know if the average number of faults is within the prescribed limit.
- *Economics:* Policy-makers are interested in knowing if there has been any significant impact on the performance of small-scale industries due to the opening up of the economy.
- *Research:* A scientist wants to know if the average output from genetically modified seeds is more than that from the normal variety of seed.

2.4.1 Type I and Type II Errors

While testing a hypothesis, if we reject it when it should be accepted, it amounts to *Type I* error. On the other hand, accepting a hypothesis when it should be rejected amounts to *Type II* error. Generally, any attempt to reduce one type of error results in increasing the other type of error. The only way to reduce both types of errors is to increase the sample size.

2.4.2 Significance Level (*p*-value)

There is always a probabilistic component involved in the accept-reject decision in testing hypothesis. The criterion that is used for accepting or rejecting a null hypothesis is called significance level or *p*-value.

The *p*-value represents the probability of concluding (incorrectly) that there is a difference in your samples when no true difference exists. It is a statistic calculated by comparing the distribution of given sample data and an expected distribution (normal, F, *t*, etc.) and is dependent upon the statistical test being performed. For example, if two samples are being compared in a *t*-test, a *p*-value of 0.05 means that there is only 5% chance of arriving at the calculated *t*-value if the samples were not different (from the same population). In other words, a *p*-value of 0.05 means there is only a 5% chance that you would be wrong in concluding that the populations are different or 95% confident of making a right decision. For social sciences research, a *p*-value of 0.05 is generally taken as standard.

2.4.3 One-Tailed and Two-Tailed Tests

A directional hypothesis is tested with a one-tailed test whereas a non-directional hypothesis is tested with a two-tailed test.

The following three relationships are only possible between any two parameters, μ_1 and μ_2:

(*a*) $\mu_1 = \mu_2$
(*b*) $\mu_1 < \mu_2$
(*c*) $\mu_1 > \mu_2$

To be able to formulate mutually exclusive and exhaustive null and alternative hypotheses from these relations we can choose either (b) or (c) as alternative hypothesis and combine one of these two with (a) to formulate the null hypothesis. Thus we will have H_0 and H_1 as:

H_0: $\mu_1 \geq \mu_2$ or $\mu_1 \leq \mu_2$
H_1: $\mu_1 < \mu_2$ or $\mu_1 > \mu_2$

The above hypotheses are called directional hypotheses and one-tailed tests are done for their analysis. If our null hypothesis is given by (a) only and (b) and (c) are combined to formulate alternative hypothesis, we will have the following H_0 and H_1:

H_0: $\mu_1 = \mu_2$
H_1: $\mu_1 \neq \mu_2$

The above hypotheses are called non-directional, as we are only concerned about the equality or non-directional inequality of the relationship. A two-tailed test is done for testing such hypotheses.

The null hypothesis is rejected if the *p*-value obtained is less than and accepted if it is greater than the significance level at which we are testing the hypothesis. Most of the times, our objective is to reject the null hypothesis and find support for our alternate hypothesis. Therefore we look for *p* values to be less than 0.05 (the commonly used significance level).

3

Summarizing Data: Descriptive Statistics

A manager in his day-to-day operations requires as much information as possible about the business performance, economic environment and industry trends to be able to make the right decisions. With the advancement in the field of information and communication technologies, it has become much easier to capture data and a huge amount of data is available with the organizations. However, the sheer amount of data makes it virtually impossible to comprehend it in its raw form. Descriptive statistics are used to summarize and present this data in a meaningful manner so that the underlying information is easily understood.

This chapter presents some of the tools for summarizing various kinds of data with the help of SPSS and MS Excel. Some basic terms and concepts have also been briefly explained but the emphasis is in explaining the use of a software package for summarizing data. Readers should refer to some standard textbook on statistics to get details about the concepts.

3.1 BASIC CONCEPTS

Descriptive statistics are numerical and graphical methods used to summarize data and bring forth the underlying information. The numerical methods include measures of central tendency and measures of variability.

3.1.1 Measures of Central Tendency

Measures of central tendency provide information about a representative value of the data set. Arithmetic mean (simply called the mean), median and mode are the most common measures of central tendency.

1. **Mean** or average is the sum of the values of a variable divided by the number of observations.
2. **Median** is a point in the data set above and below which half of the cases fall.
3. **Mode** is the most frequently occurring value in a data set.

Which of the above should be used in a particular case is a judgement call. For example, business schools regularly publish the mean salary of their passing out batches every year. However, there may be some outliers in the salary data on the upper side, which will drive the mean level towards the upper side. Thus in a class of 50 students, if two students manage to get salaries to the tune of Rs 5 million per annum, and the mean of the remaining 48 students is 200,000 per annum, the mean of the entire class will be about Rs 400,000 per annum, almost double! Clearly, the mean does not tell much about the average salary an aspiring student should expect after passing out from the school. In such a case, the median may be a better measure of central tendency. Therefore, only knowing a particular measure of central tendency may not be sufficient to make any sense of the data as it does not provide any information about the spread of the data. We use measures of variability for this purpose.

3.1.2 Measures of Variability

Measures of variability provide information about the amount of spread or dispersion among the variables. Range, variance and standard deviation are the common measures of variability.

1. **Range** is the difference between the largest and the smallest value.
2. **Variance** is the sum of the squared deviations of each value from the mean divided by the number of observations. **Standard deviation** is the positive square root of variance.

Some other important terms are explained below:

3.1.3 Percentiles, Quartiles and Interquartile Range

Percentiles and quartiles are used to find the relative standing of values in a data set. The nth percentile is a number such that n% of the values are at or below this number. Median is the 50th percentile or the 2nd quartile. Similarly, the 1st quartile is the 25th percentile and the 3rd quartile is the 75th percentile.

Interquartile range is the difference between values at the 3rd quartile (or 75th percentile) and the 1st quartile (or 25th percentile).

3.1.4 Skewness

Besides mean, median and mode, it is also important to know if the given distribution is symmetric or not. A distribution is said to be skewed if the observations above and below the mean are not symmetrically distributed. A zero value of skewness implies a symmetric distribution. The distribution is positively skewed when the mean is greater than the median and negatively skewed when the mean is less than the median. Figure 3.1 shows a positively and negatively skewed distribution.

Figure 3.1
Negatively and Positively Skewed Distributions

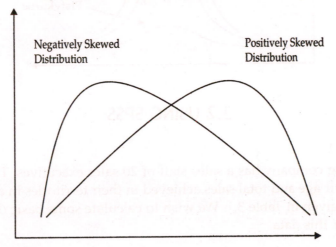

3.1.5 Kurtosis

Kurtosis is a measure of how peaked or flat a distribution is. A distribution could be mesokurtic, leptokurtic or platykurtic.

The absolute value of kurtosis for a **mesokurtic** or normal distribution is 3; kurtosis for other distributions is always measured relative to this value. **Platykurtic** distribution has a negative kurtosis, implying a flatter distribution than the normal distribution while **leptokurtic** distribution has positive kurtosis, implying a more peaked distribution than normal distribution. Figure 3.2 presents a sketch of the above three types of distributions:

Next, we show how to calculate these statistics using the SPSS program.

Figure 3.2
Meso, Lepto and Platykurtic Distributions

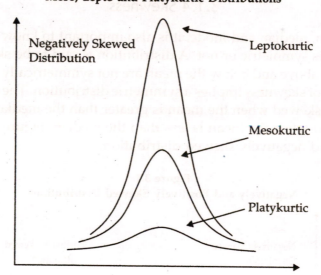

3.2 USING SPSS

Example 3.1

A marketing company has a sales staff of 20 sales executives. The data regarding their age and total sales achieved in their territories in a particular month are given in Table 3.1. We wish to calculate some basic des-criptive statistics for this data.

Table 3.1

Sales Executives	Gender (M=1, F=2)	Age	Region	Sales (in Rs '000)
1	1	25	1	50
2	1	22	1	75
3	1	20	2	11
4	1	27	2	77
5	1	28	3	45
6	1	24	1	52
7	1	24	2	26
8	1	23	3	24
9	2	24	3	28
10	2	30	3	31
11	2	19	2	36
12	2	24	1	72
13	2	26	1	69
14	2	26	1	51
15	2	21	2	34
16	2	24	2	40
17	2	29	3	18
18	2	27	3	35
19	2	24	1	29
20	2	25	1	68

Various options for calculating descriptive statistics can be found in the *Descriptive Statistics* option and *Tables* option under the *Analyze* menu as shown in Figure 3.3. We will explain their use one by one.

3.2.1 Descriptive Statistics

The first step is to enter the given data in the data editor. The variables are labeled as *executiv, gender, age, region* and *sales* respectively. Click on *Analyze*, which will produce a drop down menu, choose *Descriptive Statistics* from that and click on *Descriptives* as shown in Figure 3.3. The resulting dialogue box is shown in Figure 3.4.

In this dialogue box, we have to select the variables for which we wish to calculate descriptive statistics by transferring them to the *Variable(s)* box on the right-hand side from the left-hand side box. For this, first highlight the

Figure 3.3

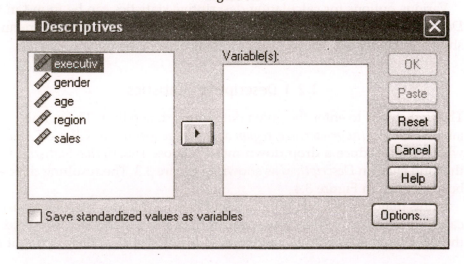

Figure 3.4

variable(s) by clicking on them (the first one—*executiv* is already high-lighted). Then, click on the arrow button between the two boxes. The high-lighted variable will get transferred to the other box. The same can also be done by double clicking on the variable, which we wish to transfer. Many dialogue boxes for specifying procedures in SPSS in the next chapters will be similar to this one in many respects.

In our example, we will transfer *age* and *sales* to the *Variable(s)* box for calculating descriptive statistics about these two. There is a button labeled *Option* at the right-hand bottom of the dialogue box. Clicking on this will produce the dialogue box shown in Figure 3.5.

Figure 3.5

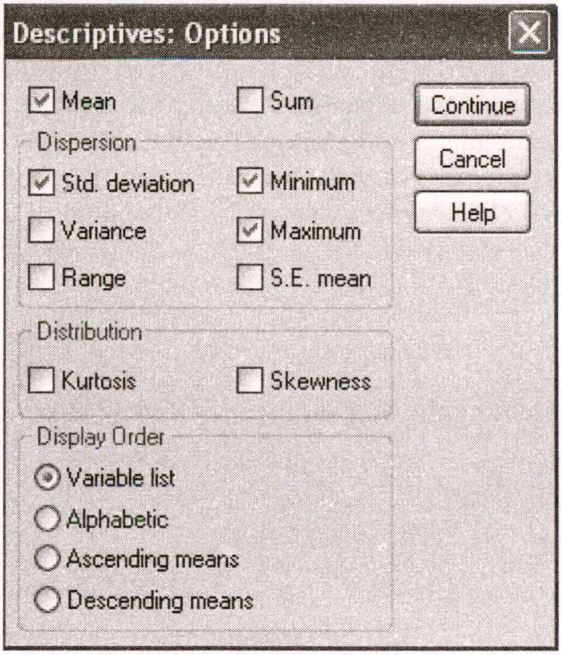

There are some default selections made in this box about the statistics to be shown in the output. A particular statistic can be selected or deselected for display in the output by clicking on the boxes next to their names. We have not selected any additional statistics other than what is selected by default. Now click on the *Continue* button to return to the previous dialogue box and then click on *OK* to run the analysis.

Output

The output produced is shown in Figure 3.6.

Figure 3.6

Descriptives

Descriptive Statistics

	N	Minimum	Maximum	Mean	Std. Deviation
age	20	19.00	30.00	24.6000	2.83586
sales	20	11.00	77.00	43.5500	19.97492
Valid N (listwise)	20				

The first line tells us about the data set for which descriptive statistics have been calculated. The first column in the output table, labeled *N* gives the number of cases in the data set. In the next two columns, the minimum and maximum value of the variables selected for analysis is given. In the last two columns, the mean and standard deviation are given.

It can be seen that the age of the sales executives vary from 19 to 30 years with a mean age of 24.6 years and a standard deviation of 2.84 years. Similarly, the sale achieved varies from Rs 11,000 to Rs 77,000 with a mean sales of Rs 43,550 and standard deviation of Rs 19,970.

SYNTAX

The syntax for obtaining the above output is given below:

DESCRIPTIVES
VARIABLES = age sales
/STATISTICS = MEAN STDDEV MIN MAX.

3.2.2 Frequencies

As shown in Figure 3.3, the *Frequencies* option can be found under *Analyze* from the menu bar. The resulting dialogue box is shown in Figure 3.7.

Transfer age from the left-hand side box to the *Variable(s)* box on the right-hand side for analysis. For transferring variables, first highlight them one by one by clicking on them. Then click on the arrow button between the two boxes to transfer the highlighted variable to the other box. Here, we have selected only age for illustration.

Figure 3.7

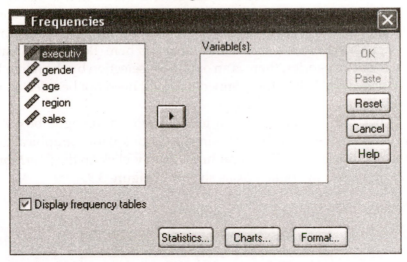

Clicking on *OK* would produce frequency tables for all the variables in the *Variable(s)* box. However, we may display some other descriptive statistics in the output. Click on the *Statistics* button at the bottom of the box to get the dialogue box (Figure 3.8).

Figure 3.8

There are a variety of descriptive statistics mentioned in this dialogue box under four categories—*percentile values, central tendency, dispersion* and *distribution*. All the statistics under central tendency, dispersion and distribution categories are selected for analyses here. Besides the statistics under the four categories, there is an option for selection by the name *Values are group midpoints*. This is for grouped data and need not be selected in our example.

Now, click on *Continue* to return to the previous dialogue box. At this stage, we can run the analysis by clicking on *OK* or opt for a graphical display of frequency distribution. For a graphical display, click on the *Charts* button; this will produce a dialogue box as shown in Figure 3.9.

Figure 3.9

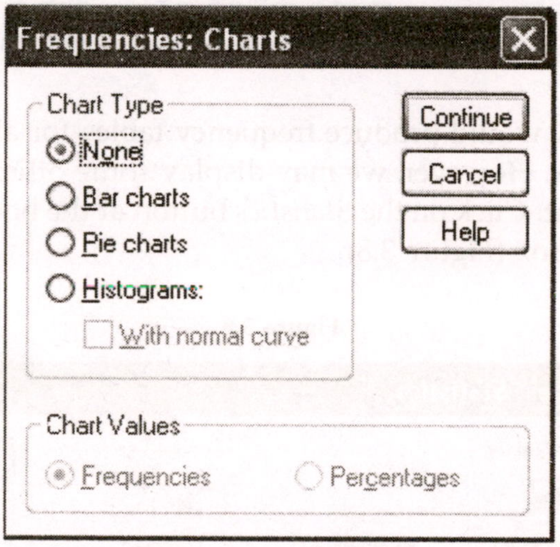

Select the type of chart you wish to show in the output and click on *Continue* to return to the main dialogue box. For our example, we have opted for bar charts since the variables under study have only small number of values. For variables with large number of values, histograms are preferred. Click on *OK* on the main dialogue box to run the analysis.

Output

The output produced is shown in three heads—frequencies, frequency table, and bar chart in Figures 3.10, 3.11 and 3.12 respectively.

SPSS output produces all the descriptive statistics requested for the selected variables as shown in Figure 3.10. The details about these statistics have been given at the beginning of the chapter. It also produces frequency distribution for each variable. In Figure 3.11, we have shown the frequency distribution output only for *Age*. The first column of the frequency table lists all the values found for the variable; the second column titled *Frequency* lists the number of data points having that value; the third column titled *Percent* gives the percentage of all data points having that particular value; the fourth column titled *Valid Percent* gives the percentage of all valid data points on this variable; and the fifth column gives the cumulative percentage for that value.

Figure 3.12 shows the bar chart of the output for the variable *Age*. On the horizontal axis are shown the values and on vertical axis, their frequencies. Much advanced graphical display of data can be done in SPSS under the *Graph* option from the menu bar.

Figure 3.10

Frequencies

Statistics

age

N	Valid	20
	Missing	0
Mean		24.6000
Std. Error of Mean		.63412
Median		24.0000
Mode		24.00
Std. Deviation		2.83586
Variance		8.042
Skewness		-.070
Std. Error of Skewness		.512
Kurtosis		-.093
Std. Error of Kurtosis		.992
Range		11.00
Minimum		19.00
Maximum		30.00
Sum		492.00

Figure 3.11

age

		Frequency	Percent	Valid Percent	Cumulative Percent
Valid	19.00	1	5.0	5.0	5.0
	20.00	1	5.0	5.0	10.0
	21.00	1	5.0	5.0	15.0
	22.00	1	5.0	5.0	20.0
	23.00	1	5.0	5.0	25.0
	24.00	6	30.0	30.0	55.0
	25.00	2	10.0	10.0	65.0
	26.00	2	10.0	10.0	75.0
	27.00	2	10.0	10.0	85.0
	28.00	1	5.0	5.0	90.0
	29.00	1	5.0	5.0	95.0
	30.00	1	5.0	5.0	100.0
	Total	20	100.0	100.0	

Figure 3.12

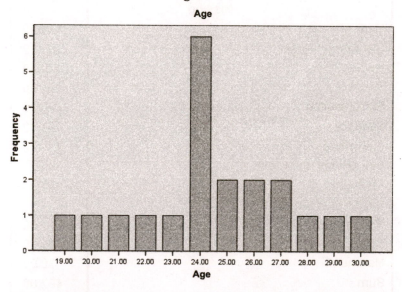

Age

SYNTAX

The syntax for obtaining the above output is given below:

    FREQUENCIES
    VARIABLES = age
    /STATISTICS = STDDEV VARIANCE RANGE MINIMUM
    MAXIMUM SEMEAN MEAN MEDIAN MODE
    SUM SKEWNESS SESKEW KURTOSIS SEKURT
    /BARCHART FREQ
    /ORDER = ANALYSIS.

3.2.3 Tables

We cannot obtain descriptive statistics for different groups of variables using either *Descriptives* or *Frequencies*. For example, in the above case if want to find out the descriptive statistics for the male and female sales executives, we have to *split* the file which can be done from the data menu. However, the tables command can still be used to produce descriptive statistics broken down by one or more categorical variables.

From the menu bar, click on *Analyze,* and select *Basic tables* from the *Tables* option. The resulting dialogue box is shown in Figure 3.13.

Select the variable for which you want to produce the descriptive statistics and transfer into the box labeled *Summaries*. There are three more boxes labeled *Down, Across,* and *Separate Tables* below *Summaries* in the Figure 3.13. The categorical variables by which the groups are to be formed, have to be moved to one of these boxes. Which box to choose for moving the grouping variable will depend on the way you want your tables to be produced. The *Down* option will produce a separate row whereas the *Across* option will produce a separate column for each level of the categorical variable. The *Separate Tables* option will produce a separate table for each level of the categorical variable.

In this example we transfer *age* to the box labeled *Summaries* and *gender* to the box labeled *Down.* Readers are encouraged to explore other options. Click on the button labeled *Statistics.* This will produce a dialogue box labeled *Basic Tables: Statistics* (Figure 3.14).

Select the statistics you want for the data from the box labeled *Statistics* on the left-hand side. Selecting any one statistic will turn the button labeled

Figure 3.13

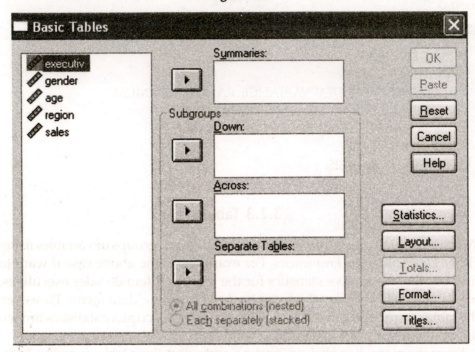

Figure 3.14

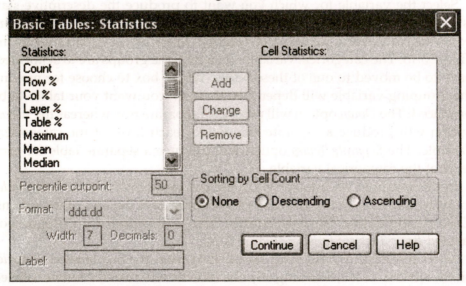

Add active. Click on *Add* to transfer the required statistic to the box labeled *Cell Statistics.* You can remove a particular statistic from this box by clicking on the *Remove* button, which becomes active only when there is at least one statistic transferred to the *Cell Statistics* box. For our example, we will choose *Maximum, Mean, Median, Minimum* and *Mode.* There are a variety of other options on these dialogue boxes by which one can choose the layout and appearance of the output. Readers are encouraged to experiment with these options and discover how they work. Click on *Continue* to return to the previous dialogue box and click on *OK* to run the analysis.

Output

The output produced is shown in Figure 3.15. It is self explanatory.

Figure 3.15

Tables

	Maximum	Mean	Median	Minimum	Mode
Female	28.00	24.13	24.00	20.00	24.00
Male	30.00	24.92	24.50	19.00	24.00

SYNTAX

The syntax for obtaining the above output is given below:

```
TABLES
/FORMAT BLANK MISSING('.')
/OBSERVATION age
/TABLES gender > age
BY (STATISTICS)
/STATISTICS
maximum( )
mean( )
median( )
minimum( )
mode( ).
```

4

Comparing Means:
One or Two Samples *t*-Tests

t-tests and *z*-tests are commonly used when making comparisons between the means of two samples or between some standard value and the mean of one sample. There are different varieties of *t*-tests which are used in different conditions depending on the design of the experiment or the nature of the data. These are explained in detail in the following sections.

4.1 BASIC CONCEPTS

4.1.1 *t*-test and *z*-test

t-tests are similar to commonly encountered *z*-tests in many ways. Both *z*- and *t*-tests have the same rationale but use different assumptions, which require a careful selection depending on the requirements. For *z*-tests, the population mean and population standard deviation should be known exactly. In many real life problems, while the population mean is known, the exact population standard deviation can't be calculated. In such cases, *t*-tests should be used. Besides, the *t*-test does not require a big sample size. Most statisticians feel that with a sample size of 30–40, results of the *t*-test are very close to those obtained from the *z*-test.

There are three different types of *t*-tests: one sample *t*-test, independent samples *t*-test and dependent (paired) samples *t*-test. Each of these is explained below.

4.1.2 One Sample *t*-test

One sample *t*-test is used to compare the mean of a single sample with the population mean. Some situations where one sample *t*-test can be used are given below:

- An economist wants to know if the per capita income of a particular region is same as the national average.
- A market researcher wants to know if the proposed product will be able to penetrate to a certain level in the households in order to make its introduction profitable.
- The Quality Control department wants to know if the mean dimensions of a particular product have shifted significantly away from the original specifications.

4.1.3 Independent Samples *t*-test

In many real life situations, we cannot determine the exact value of the population mean. We are only interested in comparing two populations using a random sample from each. Such experiments, where we are interested in detecting differences between the means of two independent groups are called independent samples test. Some situations where independent samples *t*-test can be used are given below:

- An economist wants to compare the per capita income of two different regions.
- A market researcher wants to know in which territory will his product be able to penetrate more. This will help him in deciding the right place to introduce the product.
- A labor union wants to compare the productivity levels of workers for two different groups.
- An aspiring MBA student wants to compare the salaries offered to the graduates of two business schools.

In all the above examples, the purpose is to compare between two independent groups in contrast to determining if the mean of the group exceeds a specific value as in the case of one sample *t*-tests.

4.1.4 Dependent (Paired) Samples *t*-test

In case of independent samples test for testing the difference between means, we assume that the observations on one sample are not dependent on the other. However, this assumption limits the scope of analysis as in many cases the study has to be done on the same set of elements (people, objects etc.) to control some of the sample specific extraneous factors. Such experiments where the observations are made on the same sample at two different times, is called dependent or paired sample *t*-test. Some situations where dependent samples *t*-test can be used are given below:

- The HR manager wants to know if a particular training program had any impact in increasing the motivation level of the employees.
- The Production manager wants to know if a new method of handling machines helps in reducing the break down period.
- An educationist wants to know if interactive teaching helps students learn more as compared to one-way lecturing.

One can compare these cases with the previous ones to observe the difference. The subjects in all these cases are the same and observations are taken at two different times.

4.2 USING SPSS

Various options for different types of *t*-tests can be found in the *Compare Means* option under the *Analyze* menu as shown in Figure 4.1. We will explain the procedure for the three types of *t*-tests one by one.

4.2.1 One Sample *t*-test

Example 4.1

A business school in its advertisements claims that the average salary of its graduates in a particular lean year is at par with the average salaries offered at the top five business schools. A sample of 30 graduates, from the business school whose claim was to be verified, was taken at random. Their salaries are given in Table 4.1.

Table 4.1

Graduate Student	Salary (in Rs '000)	Graduate Student	Salary (in Rs '000)
1	750	16	770
2	600	17	680
3	600	18	670
4	650	19	740
5	700	20	760
6	780	21	775
7	860	22	845
8	810	23	870
9	780	24	640
10	670	25	690
11	690	26	715
12	550	27	630
13	610	28	685
14	715	29	780
15	755	30	635

Figure 4.1

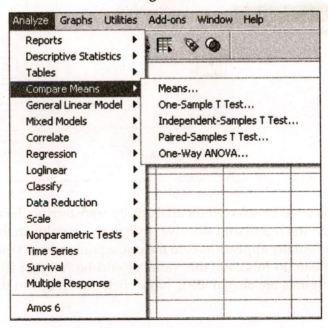

The average salary offered at the top five business schools in that year was given as Rs 750,000.

In this problem we want to assess validity of the claim made by the business school in its advertisements. We want to know if the average salary of the business school is significantly different from Rs 750,000, the average salary at the top five business schools for that particular year. The null hypothesis would be:

H_0: There is no difference between the average salary of the business school in question and the average salary of the top five business schools.

As explained earlier, the first step is to enter the given data in the data editor. The variables are labeled as *student* and *salary* respectively. Click on *Analyze*, which will produce a drop down menu, choose *Compare Means* from that and click on *One-sample T test...*as shown in Figure 4.1. The resulting dialogue box is shown in Figure 4.2.

Figure 4.2

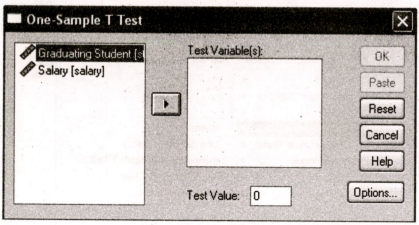

The variables can be selected for analysis by transferring them to the *Test Variable* box on the right-hand side. Next, change the value in the *Test Value* box, which originally appears as 0, to the one against which you are testing the sample mean. In this case, this value would be 750 (not 750,000, since other salary figures are also in '000). Now click on *OK* to run the analysis.

Output

The output produced is shown in Figure 4.3.

Figure 4.3

T-Test

One-Sample Statistics

	N	Mean	Std. Deviation	Std. Error Mean
Salary	30	713.50	81.263	14.837

One-Sample Test

	Test Value = 750					
					95% Confidence Interval of the Difference	
	t	df	Sig. (2-tailed)	Mean Difference	Lower	Upper
Salary	-2.460	29	.020	-36.500	-66.84	-6.16

The first table, labeled *One-Sample Statistics*, gives descriptive statistics for the variable *salary*. The second table, labeled *One-Sample Test*, gives the results of the *t*-test analysis. The first entry is the value of the *t*-statistic, next is the degrees of freedom (df), followed by the corresponding p value for 2-tailed test given as *Sig. (2-tailed)*.

The test result gives the *t*-statistic of –2.46 with 29 degrees of freedom. The corresponding two-tailed p value is 0.02. If we take the significance level of 5%, we can see that the p value obtained is less than 0.05. Therefore, we can reject the null hypothesis at $\alpha = 0.05$, which means that the sample mean is significantly different from the hypothesized value and the average salary of the business school in question is not the same as the average salary of the top five business schools at the 5% level of significance.

However, at $\alpha = 0.01$ the null hypothesis will have to be accepted since the p-value is greater than 0.01. This means that at 1% level of significance, the claim of the business school that its salaries are same as that of the top five business schools is right.

The second output window also gives the mean difference (the difference between sample mean and the hypothesized value) and the interval limits at the specified values of the confidence level. These figures are not of much use for practical considerations.

SPSS does not give the one-tailed significance value directly, however, one can compute the one-tailed value by dividing the two-tailed value by 2.

SYNTAX

The syntax for obtaining the above output is given below:

```
T-TEST
/TESTVAL=750
/MISSING=ANALYSIS
/VARIABLES=salary
/CRITERIA=CIN (.95).
```

4.2.2 Independent Samples t-test

Example 4.2

A study was conducted to compare the efficiency of the workers of two mines, one with private ownership and the other with government ownership. The researcher was of the view that there is no significant difference in their efficiency levels. Total tonnage of the mineral mined by a worker in one shift was chosen as the criteria to assess his efficiency.

20 workers from the private sector mine and 24 from the government-owned mine were selected and their average output per shift was recorded. The data obtained is given in Table 4.2.

In this problem we want to assess whether the efficiency of the workers of the two mines is the same. The null hypothesis in this case would be that there is no difference in the efficiency of the workers of the two mines.

H_0: Average output of the workers from mine 1 equals that of the workers from mine 2.

The alternative hypothesis in this case would be that the workers of the two mines significantly differ in their efficiency, i.e., average output of workers of mine 1 is significantly different from that of the workers of mine 2.

The variables are labeled as *miner*, *mine* and *output* respectively for entering into the SPSS Program. Click on *Analyze*, which will produce a drop down menu, choose *Compare Means* from that and click on *Independent-Samples T Test* as shown in Figure 4.1. The resultant dialogue box is shown in Figure 4.4.

Table 4.2

Miner	Mine	Output (in tones)	Miner	Mine	Output (in tones)
1	1	48	23	2	41
2	1	45	24	2	39
3	1	33	25	2	35
4	1	39	26	2	34
5	1	34	27	2	33
6	1	49	28	2	36
7	1	33	29	2	37
8	1	45	30	2	37
9	1	48	31	2	41
10	1	44	32	2	42
11	1	45	33	2	39
12	1	45	34	2	38
13	1	36	35	2	38
14	1	48	36	2	39
15	1	41	37	2	41
16	1	47	38	2	40
17	1	39	39	2	41
18	1	49	40	2	40
19	1	38	41	2	38
20	1	45	42	2	41
21	2	42	43	2	43
22	2	44	44	2	40

Figure 4.4

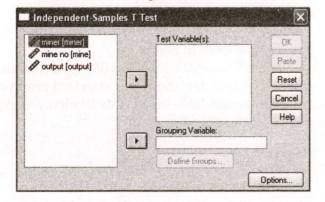

Initially all the variables are shown in the left-hand box. To perform the Independent-Samples *t*-test, transfer the dependent variable(s) into the *Test Variable(s)* box and transfer the variable that identifies the groups into the *Grouping Variable* box. In this case *output* is the dependent variable to be analyzed and should be transferred into *Test Variable(s)* box by clicking on the first arrow in the middle of the two boxes. *Mine* is the variable which will identify the groups of the miners and it should be transferred into the *Grouping Variable* box.

Once the Grouping Variable is transferred, the *Define Groups* button which was earlier inactive turns active. Clicking on it will produce a box shown in Figure 4.5.

Figure 4.5

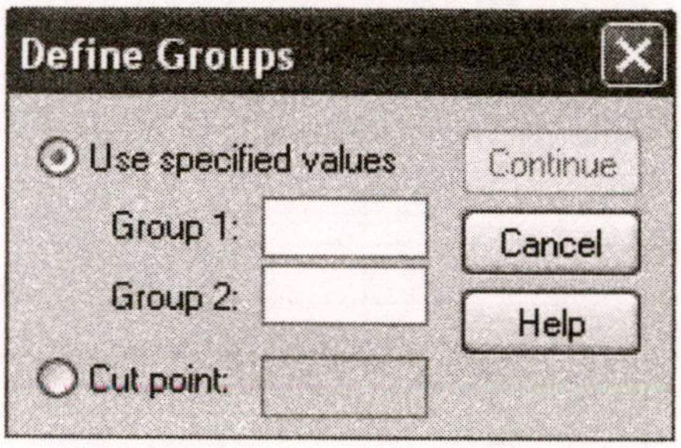

In the example *Group 1* represents the miners of mine 1 and *Group 2* represents the miners of mine 2, which we have entered under the variable *mine* in the data editor. Therefore, put *1* in the box against *Group 1* and put *2* in the box against *Group 2* and click *Continue*. Now click on *OK* to run the test.

Output

The output produced is shown in Figure 4.6

The first table, labeled *Group Statistics* gives descriptive statistics (number of data sets, means, standard deviations and standard errors of means) for both the groups. The second table below this labeled *Independent-Sample Test* gives the results of the analysis.

Figure 4.6

T-Test

Group Statistics

	mine no	N	Mean	Std. Deviation	Std. Error Mean
output	1	20	42.5500	5.48179	1.22577
	2	24	39.1250	2.78681	.56886

Independent Samples Test

		Levene's Test for Equality of Variances		t-test for Equality of Means						95% Confidence Interval of the Difference	
		F	Sig.	t	df	Sig. (2-tailed)	Mean Difference	Std. Error Difference		Lower	Upper
output	Equal variances assumed	16.031	.000	2.678	42	.011	3.42500	1.27905		.84377	6.00623
	Equal variances not assumed			2.535	27.030	.017	3.42500	1.35133		.65244	6.19756

In this table we get results of the two tests—*Levene's Test for Equality of Variances* and *t-test for Equality of Means*. The table contains two sets of analysis, the first one assuming equal variances in the two groups and the second one assuming unequal variances. The Levene's test tells us which statistic to consider to analyze the equality of the means. It tests the null hypothesis that the two groups have equal variances. A small value of significance associated with Levene's test indicates that the two groups have unequal variances and the null hypothesis is false. In the given example, a very small value of this test statistic indicates that the two groups, *Mine 1* and *Mine 2*, do not have equal variance. Therefore, the statistic associated with *equal variances not assumed* should be used for the *t*-test for Equality of Means.

The *t*-test result (with equal variances not assumed) shows *t* statistic of 2.535 with 27.03 degrees of freedom. The corresponding two-tailed *p*-value is 0.017, which is less than 0.05 but higher than 0.01. Therefore, we can reject the null hypothesis at 5% significance level, which means that the average outputs of the two mines are significantly different from each other, i.e., the miners of the two mines do not have the same efficiency. However at 1% significance level, the null hypothesis will have to be accepted since the p-value is greater than 0.01. This means that at 1% significance level, the claim that the efficiency of the miners of the two mines is same is right.

The table also gives the mean difference, i.e., the difference between the average daily output by the workers of mine 1 and mine 2, standard error of difference and 95% confidence interval of the difference. While the mean difference helps in observing the total amount of difference between the mean values for the two groups, the other two values are not of much importance for practical purposes.

One-tailed and Two-tailed Tests

We may recall the hypotheses we tested above:

H_0: O1 = O2
H_1: O1 ≠ O2

Here we are only interested in knowing if the efficiency of the workers of mine 1 is same as that of the workers of mine 2. The appropriate test for this would be a two-tailed test. However, if we were to test the assumption that the efficiency of workers of mine 1 is greater than that of the workers of mine 2, the null and alternative hypotheses would be different and we would need the p-value of one-tailed test. The new hypotheses would be:

H_0: O1 ≤ O2
H_1: O1 > O2

The one-tailed significance value or p-value can be obtained by dividing the two-tailed value by two. Thus the one-tailed p-value in this case would be 0.0085, which is less than 0.01. Therefore we reject the null hypothesis even at 1% significance level and conclude that the efficiency of the workers of mine 1 is greater than that of the workers of mine 2.

SYNTAX

The syntax for obtaining the above output is given below:

```
T-TEST
GROUPS=mine(1 2)
/MISSING=ANALYSIS
/VARIABLES=output
/CRITERIA=CIN(.95).
```

4.2.3 Dependent Samples *t*-test

Example 4.3

A corporate training institution claimed that its training program can greatly enhance the efficiency of call center employees. A big call center sent some of its employees for the training program. The efficiency was measured by the number of deals closed by each employee in a one-month period. Data was collected for a one-month period before sending the employees for the training program. After the training program, data was again collected on the same employees for a one-month period. The data is given in Table 4.3.

Table 4.3

Employee	Before Training Program	After Training Program	Employee	Before Training Program	After Training Program
1	41	44	11	46	39
2	35	36	12	42	40
3	40	48	13	37	36
4	50	47	14	34	39
5	39	40	15	38	50
6	45	52	16	42	46
7	35	35	17	46	49
8	36	51	18	39	42
9	44	46	19	40	51
10	40	55	20	45	37

In this problem, we want to test the validity of the claim made by the training institution that its training program improves the efficiency of call center employees. We want to know if there is a significant difference in the average output of the employees before and after going through the training program.

The null hypothesis here would be that the average output of the employees is same before and after going through the training program.

The given data is entered in the data editor and the variables are labeled as *employee*, *before*, and *after* respectively. Click on *Analyze*, which will produce a drop down menu, choose *Compare Means* from that and click on *Paired-Samples T test* as shown in Figure 4.1. The resulting dialogue box is shown in Figure 4.7.

Figure 4.7

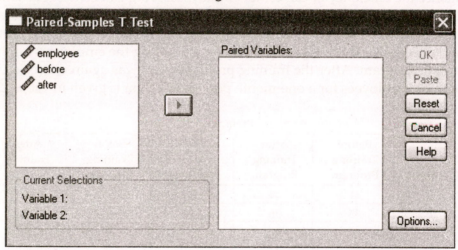

The variables appear in the left-hand box. From this box we have to select the variables, which are to be compared. The two variables to be compared in our case are *before* and *after*. Select these together and they will immediately appear in the box at the bottom labeled *Current Selection*. They are simultaneously highlighted in the box in which they originally appeared. Once the variables are selected, the arrow at the center becomes active. The variables can be transferred to the *Paired Variables* box by clicking on this arrow. They will appear in the *Paired Variables* box as *before–after*. Now click on *OK* to run the analysis.

Output

The output produced is shown in Figure 4.8 in three tables. The first table labeled *Paired Samples Statistics* gives descriptive statistics (means, number of data sets, standard deviations and standard errors of means) for both, *before* and *after* situations. The second table labeled *Paired Samples Correlations* gives the value of the correlation coefficient between the two variables and significance level for the two-tailed test to assess the hypothesis that the correlation coefficient equals zero. This has been explained in detail in Chapter 7.

The third table labeled *Paired Samples Test* gives the results of the analysis. The statistics given under the label *Paired Differences* are calculated by computing the differences between the paired values (in this case by subtracting the *after* variable from the *before* variable). The mean, standard deviation and standard error of mean of these differences along with 95% confidence interval for the mean of differences are given here. Next to this are given the results of the *t*-test. The test results show a *t*-statistic of -3.004 with 19 degrees of freedom. The two-tailed *p*-value is 0.007, which is less than the conventional 5% or 1% level of significance. Therefore, we can reject the null hypothesis at 5% (or 1%) significance level, which means that the average output of the employees has indeed changed after attending the training program.

SYNTAX

The syntax for obtaining the above output is given below:

```
T-TEST
PAIRS=before WITH after (PAIRED)
/CRITERIA=CIN(.95)
/MISSING=ANALYSIS.
```

Output

The output obtained is shown in Figure 4.8 in three tables. The first table, labeled Paired Samples Statistics, gives descriptive statistics (mean, number of cases, standard deviations and standard errors of means) for both behaviour measures before and after. The second table labeled Paired Samples Correlations gives the value of the correlation coefficient between the two variables and significance of it in the two-tailed test to assess the hypothesis that the relation is different equal to zero. The test has been calculated in half the namely. The third table labeled Paired Samples Test gives the results of the analyses. The statistic given under the label Paired Differences are calculated by comparing the differences between the paired values (in this case by subtracting one variable from the base variable). The mean, standard deviation and standard errors of mean of these differences along with 95% confidence interval of the mean of differences are given here. Next to this are given results of the t-test. The test results show a t-statistic of -3.004 with 19 degrees of freedom. The two-tailed p-value is 0.007, which is less than the critical value for the 5% level of significance, therefore we can reject the null hypothesis at 5% (or 1%) significance level, which means that the drug treatment of depression has induced a significant diminishing the value of depression.

Syntax

The syntax to obtain the above output is given below.

T-TEST
    PAIRS=before WITH after (PAIRED)
    /CRITERIA=CIN(.95)
    /MISSING=ANALYSIS.

T-Test

Figure 4.8

Paired Samples Statistics

		Mean	N	Std. Deviation	Std. Error Mean
Pair 1	before	40.2000	20	4.37216	.97764
	after	44.1500	20	6.15822	1.37702

Paired Samples Correlations

		N	Correlation	Sig.
Pair 1	before & after	20	.417	.067

Paired Samples Test

	Paired Differences					t	df	Sig. (2-tailed)
				95% Confidence Interval of the Difference				
	Mean	Std. Deviation	Std. Error Mean	Lower	Upper			
Pair 1 before - after	-3.95000	5.88016	1.31484	-6.70200	-1.19800	-3.004	19	.007

5

Comparing Means: Analysis of Variance

ANOVA or Analysis of Variance is used to compare the means of more than two populations. It uncovers the main and interaction effects of classification or independent variables on one or more dependent variables. ANOVA has found extensive application in psychological research using experimental data. It can also be used in business management, especially in consumer behavior and marketing management related problems. The examples given below will help in understanding the applicability of ANOVA for solving practical problems:

- *Consumer behavior:* A researcher wants to investigate the impact of three different advertising stimuli on the shopping propensity of males and females as well as consumers of different age brackets. The dependent variable here is shopping propensity and independent variables or the factors are advertising stimuli, gender and age brackets.
- *Marketing management:* A marketing manager wants to investigate the impact of different discount schemes on the sale of three major brands of edible oil.
- *Social sciences:* A social scientist wants to predict whether the effectiveness of an AIDS awareness campaign varies depending on the geographic location, campaign media and usage of celebrities in the campaigns.

5.1 BASIC CONCEPTS

5.1.1 ANOVA Procedure

ANOVA analysis uses the F-statistic, which tests if the means of the groups, formed by one independent variable or a combination of independent variables, are significantly different. It is based on the comparison of two estimates of variances—one representing the variance within groups, often referred to as error variance; and the other representing the variance due to differences in group means. If the two variances do not differ significantly, one can believe that all the group means come from the same sampling distribution of means and there is no reason to claim that the group means differ. If, however, the group means differ more than can be accounted for due to random error, there is reason to believe that they were drawn from different sampling distributions of means. The *F*-statistic calculates the ratio between the variance due to difference between groups and the error variance.

F = Variance due to difference between groups/Error variance

The larger the *F*-ratio, the greater is the difference between groups as compared to within group differences. An *F*-ratio equal to or less than one indicates that there is no significant difference between groups and the null hypothesis is correct. If the null hypothesis (that the group means do not differ significantly) is correct, then we can conclude that the independent variables did not have an effect on the dependent variable. However, if the *F*-test proves the null hypothesis to be wrong, multiple comparison tests are used to further explore the specific relationships among different groups.

The ANOVA procedure can be used correctly if the following conditions are satisfied:

1. The dependent variable should be interval or ratio data type.
2. The populations should be normally distributed and the population variances should be equal.

5.1.2 Factors and Covariates

Factors are independent variables because of which the groups might differ significantly. There could be just one factor or more than one factor in an ANOVA analysis. The analysis, however, is very cumbersome as will be clear later in the chapter, if the number of factors goes beyond three to four. A factor may have many levels.

Factors could be fixed or random. A factor is fixed if it contains all the levels of interest, and random if the levels under study are a random sample of the possible levels that could be sampled and the goal is to make a statement regarding the larger population.

Covariates are interval-level independent variables. By entering covariates in the model, we can remove the effects of the relationship between the covariate and the dependent variable and get a more precise estimate of the amount of variance by the factors in the model.

5.1.3 Between, Within and Mixed (Between-Within) Designs

An ANOVA design can be described by specifying three things:

1) Number of factors involved in the design,
2) Number of levels of each of the factors,
3) Whether the factor is a between- or within-subjects factor.

In between-groups design, the level of factor(s) varies between the subjects of different groups so that the subjects of each group will be exposed to only one level of the factor(s). This design is conceptually similar to the independent sample design discussed in the case of *t*-tests.

In within-groups design, the level of factor(s) varies within the subjects. This is done by exposing the same subject to different levels of the factor(s) at different times. It is also referred as repeated measures design. This design is conceptually similar to the paired sample design discussed in the case of *t*-tests.

When there are both, between-groups as well as within-groups factors present in a design, it is referred to as mixed design.

5.1.4 Main Effects and Interactions

Main effect is the direct effect of a single factor or independent variable on the dependent variable. It simply compares the mean of one level of a factor with the other level(s) of that factor. Interaction effect is the combined effect of two or more factors on the dependent variable.

ANOVA designs are sometimes classified depending on the number of factors. Thus a one-way ANOVA includes a single factor which gives rise to a single main effect. In case of a two-way ANOVA, there are two main effects of two factors and one two-way interaction effect between the two factors. Likewise, in the case of a three-way ANOVA, there are three main effects of three factors, three two-way interactions and one three-way interaction. If the three factors in three-way ANOVA are X, Y and Z, then we will have three main effects of X, Y and Z, three two-way interactions X*Y, X*Z and Y*Z and one three-way interaction X*Y*Z.

As the number of factors increase in an ANOVA design, the number of interactions increases steeply. In case of a four-way ANOVA, there are four main effects, six two-way interactions, four three-way interactions, and one four-way interaction. Thus the researcher has to analyze a total of 15 results. For this reason, it is not easy to interpret results of ANOVA involving more than three to four factors. Beginners are advised to keep their experimental designs simple so as not to have more than four factors.

5.1.5 Post-Hoc Multiple Comparisons

Rejection of the null hypothesis in ANOVA only tells us that all population means are not equal. Multiple comparisons are used to assess which group means differ from which others, once the overall F-test shows that at least one difference exists. Many tests are listed under "Post-Hoc" in SPSS. Tukey HSD (honestly significant difference) test is one of the most conservative and commonly-used test and has been explained in the examples given in this chapter.

5.1.6 Contrast Analysis

Contrasts are also used to do multiple comparisons in ANOVA. Using contrasts, we may test the significance of specific differences in particular parts of the design, like testing the differences between two particular means or comparing the average of a combination of means to a particular mean. This has also been explained later in the examples.

5.2 USING SPSS

As explained earlier, one may have many ANOVA designs depending on the number of factors and levels of these factors. In the following section, we will show how to use SPSS to solve the following two basic ANOVA designs.

One-Way Between-Groups ANOVA
Two-Way Between-Groups ANOVA

The SPSS program has the following four options for carrying out the ANOVA analysis:

One-Way ANOVA
Univariate GLM
Multivariate GLM
Repeated Measure GLM

One-Way ANOVA is the generalization of the *t*-test for independent samples to situations with more than two groups. It is also known as single classification ANOVA or one-factor ANOVA. It is used to test the difference in a single dependent variable among two or more groups formed by a single independent or classification variable. It can be found under the *Compare Means* item in the *Analyze* menu by the name *One-Way ANOVA*.

The other three techniques, viz., univariate, multivariate and repeated measures are found under the *General Linear Model* in the *Analyze* menu. The *Univariate GLM* is used to assess the main and interaction effects of several independent variables on a single dependent variable. The independent variables could be fixed factors, random factors or covariates. The *Multivariate GLM* is used when we have more than one dependent variable and several independent variables. This design is also known as MANOVA. The *Repeated Measures GLM* is used when a dependent variable is measured repeatedly across a set of conditions for all the subjects of the sample. Thus it is a generalization of the *t*-test for paired samples.

5.2.1 One-Way Between-Groups ANOVA

This analysis can be carried out in two ways in SPSS—using *One-Way ANOVA* or using *Univariate GLM*. The example given below has been solved using both the methods.

Example 5.1

An oil company has introduced a new brand of gasoline in its outlets in three major metro cities. However, they are not sure how the new brand is selling at the three places since there is a lot of difference in the driving habits of people in the three metros. The company selected 10 outlets in each city and tabulated the data on an average daily sale at each of the selected outlets. The data is presented in Table 5.1. The items 1, 2 and 3 in the table represent the three metros.

Table 5.1

Outlets	Metro	Volume (in Gallons)	Outlets	Metro	Volume (in Gallons)	Outlets	Metro	Volume (in Gallons)
1	1	15.00	11	2	8.00	21	3	14.60
2	1	13.50	12	2	8.25	22	3	16.50
3	1	14.20	13	2	6.40	23	3	13.20
4	1	13.00	14	2	7.20	24	3	13.60
5	1	15.00	15	2	4.40	25	3	21.00
6	1	11.00	16	2	11.30	26	3	11.70
7	1	12.50	17	2	7.80	27	3	12.30
8	1	16.00	18	2	8.10	28	3	17.00
9	1	14.25	19	2	9.00	29	3	14.75
10	1	13.50	20	2	6.80	30	3	18.00

The null hypothesis in this case is:

H_{01}: The average sale of the new brand of gasoline is same in all the metro cities.

We will also explain multiple comparisons in this example by testing for the following null hypotheses:

H_{02}: The average sale of the new brand of gasoline in city 1 is same as that in city 2.
H_{03}: The average sale of the new brand of gasoline in city 1 is same as that in city 2 and city 3 together.

Please note the difference between H_{02}, H_{03} and H_{01}. The F-statistics obtained form ANOVA only tells us whether there is any significant difference in the mean values of the three groups, which is our H_{01}. From this, we cannot conclude anything about specific hypotheses as stated in H_{02} and H_{03}. The later two hypotheses can be tested using multiple comparisons, which have been explained in the last section.

Using One-Way ANOVA

As explained in Chapter 1, first the given data is entered in the data editor. The variables are labeled as *outlets*, *metro*, and *volume* respectively. Click on *Analyze*, which will produce a drop down menu, choose *Compare Means* from that and click on *One-Way ANOVA*. The resulting dialogue box is shown in Figure 5.1.

Figure 5.1

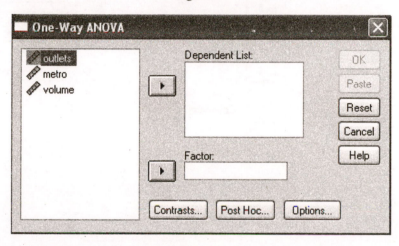

Initially, all the variables are shown in the left-hand box. To perform One-Way ANOVA, transfer the dependent variable into the box labeled *Dependent List* and the factoring variable into the box labeled *Factor*. In this case *Volume* is the dependent variable and should be transferred into the *Dependent List* box by clicking on the first arrow in the middle of the two boxes. *Metro* is the factoring variable and should be transferred into *Factor* box by clicking on the second arrow. One can select a number of additional statistics from *Options*, depending on specific requirements. The dialogue box obtained by clicking on *Options* is shown in Figure 5.3 and explained along with *Options* available in *Univariate GLM*.

Using Univariate GLM Command

Click on *Analyze*, which will produce a drop down menu, choose *General Linear Model* from that and click on *Univariate*. The resulting dialogue box is shown in Figure 5.2.

Figure 5.2

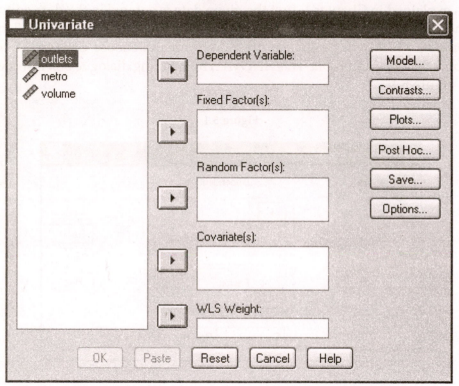

Transfer the dependent variable (volume) into the *Dependent variable* box and the factoring variable (metro) into the *Fixed Factor(s)* box. Click on *Options* to ask for additional statistics. The dialogue box obtained by clicking on *Options* is shown in Figure 5.4.

Statistically, random factors are those variables whose levels are assumed to be randomly selected from an infinite population of possible levels. Fixed factors, on the other hand, contain all of the levels of a particular variable. For example, the gender of a person could be a fixed factor if one believes

Figure 5.3

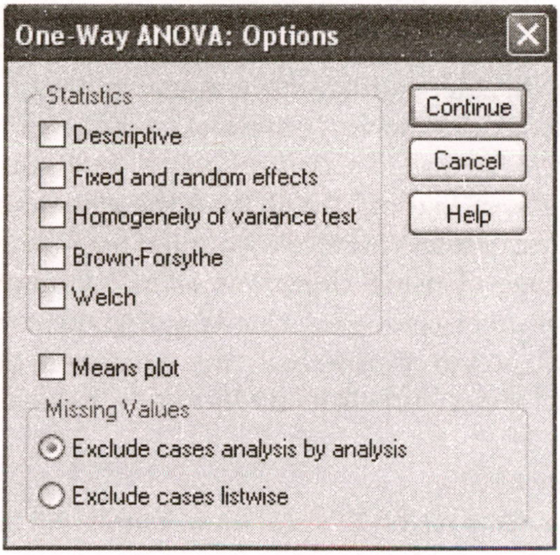

Figure 5.4

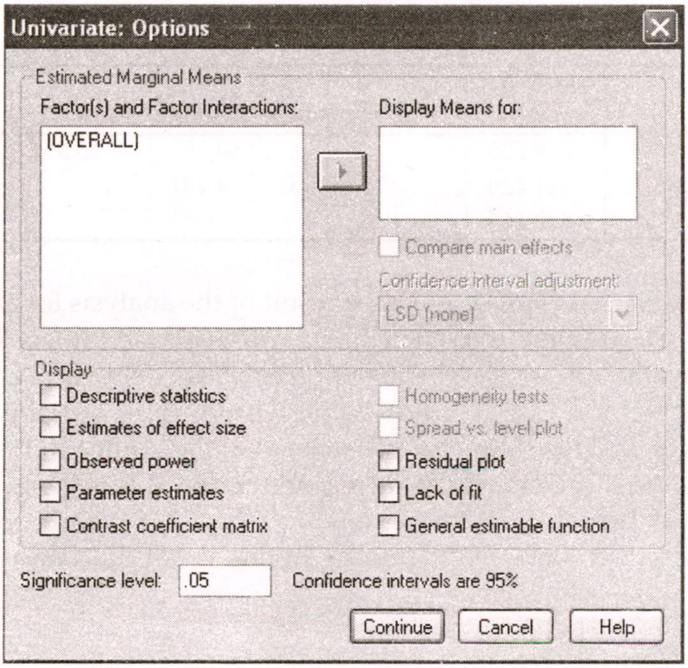

male and female to be exhaustive categories specifying gender. Age bracket or income, on the other hand is a random factor as age/income brackets may not contain exhaustive categories. The choice between random factors and fixed factors may vary depending on the research design.

One can get descriptive statistics of the data by clicking on the box opposite *Descriptive* in Figure 5.3 and *Descriptive statistics* in Figure 5.4. Clicking on *Estimates of effect size* in Figure 5.4 will give the eta-squared statistic. This gives the proportion of total variance accounted for by the factor. This is an important advantage of using *Univariate GLM* command as one cannot obtain estimates of effect sizes using *One-Way ANOVA* command. *One-Way ANOVA* command, however, does have the advantage of a much simpler output. Click on *Continue* and click on *OK* to run the analysis.

Output for One-Way ANOVA
The output for *One-Way ANOVA* is shown in Figure 5.5 labeled *Oneway*.

Figure 5.5

Oneway

volume **ANOVA**

	Sum of Squares	df	Mean Square	F	Sig.
Between Groups	319.525	2	159.762	35.524	.000
Within Groups	121.429	27	4.497		
Total	440.953	29			

The table, labeled *Oneway* gives the result of the analysis for an omnibus hypothesis. The results are given in three rows. The first row labeled *Between Groups* gives the variability due to the place of sale (between-groups variability), the second row labeled *Within Groups* gives variability due to random error, and the third row gives the total variability. In the given example, F-value is 35.524 and the corresponding p-value is given as < 0.000. Therefore we can safely reject the null hypothesis (H_{01}) and conclude that the average sale of the new brand of gasoline is not the same in all three metros.

The results will be reported as:

There is a significant difference in the sales volume of the new brand of gasoline in the three metros, $F(2, 27) = 35.52$, $p < 0.001$.

SYNTAX

The syntax for obtaining the above output is given below:

ONEWAY
volume BY metro
/MISSING ANALYSIS.

Output for Univariate GLM

The output for *Univariate GLM* is shown in Figure 5.6 labeled *Univariate Analysis of Variance*.

Figure 5.6

Univariate Analysis of Variance

Between-Subjects Factors

		N
metro	1	10
	2	10
	3	10

Tests of Between-Subjects Effects

Dependent Variable: volume

Source	Type III Sum of Squares	df	Mean Square	F	Sig.
Corrected Model	319.525ª	2	159.762	35.524	.000
Intercept	4510.454	1	4510.454	1002.911	.000
metro	319.525	2	159.762	35.524	.000
Error	121.429	27	4.497		
Total	4951.408	30			
Corrected Total	440.953	29			

a. R Squared = .725 (Adjusted R Squared = .704)

The first table labeled *Between-Subjects Factors* gives the number of subjects in each level of the factor.

The second table labeled *Tests of Between-Subjects Effects* gives the ANOVA results. The first column lists the various sources of variance. The second column gives the sum of squares of each source of variance. The *F*-value and corresponding degrees of freedom are listed in the fifth and third columns respectively. The column labeled *Mean Square* gives the mean square of each source of variance. The last column labeled *Partial Eta Squared* is obtained if we select *Estimates of effect size* from the options and it represents the size of the effect.

For the given example, the values to be paid attention to are the *F*-ratio, *df* and *p*-value corresponding to the classification variable (factor) *Metro*, and the *df* corresponding to the error term.

The results will be reported in the same manner as in the case of *One-Way ANOVA* output. The 0.725 value of partial eta squared tells us that *Metro* accounts for 72.5% of the total variance *in Volume*.

SYNTAX

The syntax for obtaining the above output is given below:

```
UNIANOVA
volume BY metro
/METHOD = SSTYPE(3)
/INTERCEPT = INCLUDE
/PRINT = ETASQ
/CRITERIA = ALPHA(.05)
/DESIGN = metro.
```

5.2.2 Unplanned and Planned Comparisons

The *F*-statistic in ANOVA only tells us that the dependent variable varies for different levels of factor(s). In case of more than two levels, the *F*-statistic does not tell us the exact way in which the dependent variable differs by the levels of factor(s). To gain a deeper understanding of the subject, we have to rely on unplanned and planned comparisons.

By unplanned comparisons, we mean exploring the differences in means between all possible pairs of groups. In the example given above, an unplanned comparison would mean that the researcher is interested in identifying whether the average sale of gasoline in a particular city is different from any other city. While making such comparisons, the researcher has no *a priori* hypotheses about differences in the dependent variable for different levels of the factor(s). Post-Hoc tests are used for such unplanned comparison.

Planned comparisons, on the other hand, are decided *a priori* by the researcher, based on theoretical considerations. Such comparisons can be done using the Contrasts analysis. A common and most frequently-used technique is to use a liner combination of contrasts. The method of assigning weights is very simple and can be learned easily with little practice.

For the example 5.1, we had three null hypotheses. We tested the first of these (H_{01}) using the *F*-statistic as illustrated earlier. The other two (H_{02} and H_{03}) are based on planned comparisons. For H_{02}, the contrasts coefficients will be –1, 1, and 0 for city 1, 2 and 3 respectively. This assignment compares the mean for city 1 with the mean for city 2. Likewise, for H_{03}, the contrasts coefficients will be 2, –1 and –1 for city 1, 2 and 3 respectively. This assignment compares the mean for city 1 with the mean for city 2 and 3 together. Essentially, if there are three factors (A, B, C), we can make the following comparisons:

1) We can compare one factor with another factor (A with B, B with C or A with C). The corresponding contrasts will be (1, –1, 0), (0, 1, –1) and (1, 0, –1).
2) We can compare one factor with the mean of the other two (A with B and C...). The corresponding contrasts will be (2, –1, –1) or (–2, 1, 1).

The assignment of contrasts will be similar if there are four factors. In the case of four factors, if we have to compare the mean of the first and third, with the mean of the second and fourth, the contrasts will be (1, –1, 1, –1). Likewise, if we have to compare the mean of the third factor with the other three, the contrast will be (–1, –1, 3, –1). One has to ensure that the comparisons are orthogonal, while performing more than one planned comparison on the same set of data. This condition is satisfied if the products of coefficients assigned to each level sum to zero.

Performing Unplanned Comparisons

To perform unplanned comparisons, click on *Post Hoc* button on the main dialogue box (Figure 5.1 in case of *One-Way ANOVA*, and Figure 5.2 in case of *Univariate GLM*). The resulting dialogue boxes appear as shown in Figures 5.7 and 5.8.

Figure 5.7

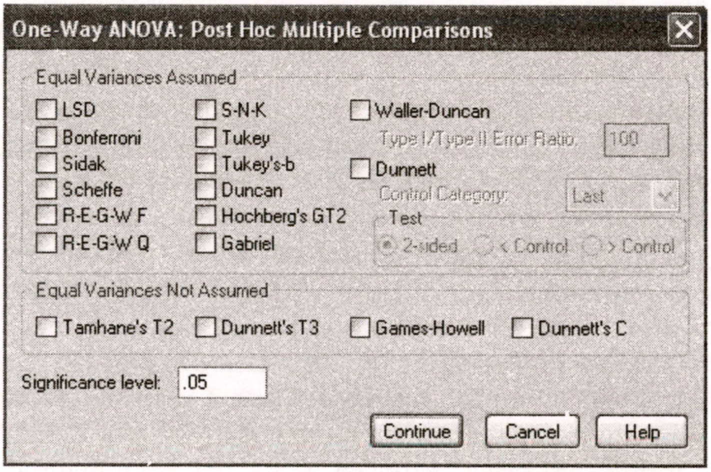

Figure 5.8

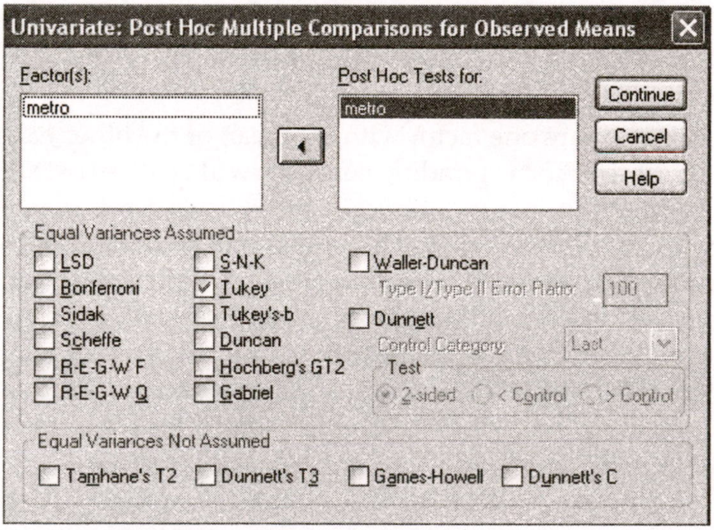

In Figure 5.8, different boxes in the bottom half of the dialogue box become active only when at least one factor is selected from the box labeled *Factor(s)* and transferred to the box labeled *Post Hoc Tests for*. One can select any of the tests mentioned in these boxes depending on how conservative one wants to be in the tests. For details on these tests, readers are advised to refer to advanced texts of statistics. We have selected *Tukey* (same as *Tukey HSD test*), as this is the most commonly reported statistic in research. Click on *Continue* and click on *OK* to run the analysis.

The output produced in both the cases is same as shown in Figure 5.9.

Figure 5.9

Post Hoc Tests

Multiple Comparisons

Dependent Variable: volume
Tukey HSD

(I) metro	(J) metro	Mean Difference (I-J)	Std. Error	Sig.	95% Confidence Interval Lower Bound	95% Confidence Interval Upper Bound
1	2	6.07000*	.94841	.000	3.7185	8.4215
	3	-1.47000	.94841	.284	-3.8215	.8815
2	1	-6.07000*	.94841	.000	-8.4215	-3.7185
	3	-7.54000*	.94841	.000	-9.8915	-5.1885
3	1	1.47000	.94841	.284	-.8815	3.8215
	2	7.54000*	.94841	.000	5.1885	9.8915

*. The mean difference is significant at the .05 level.

Homogeneous Subsets

volume

Tukey HSD[a]

metro	N	Subset for alpha = .05 — 1	Subset for alpha = .05 — 2
2	10	7.7250	
1	10		13.7950
3	10		15.2650
Sig.		1.000	.284

Means for groups in homogeneous subsets are displayed.
a. Uses Harmonic Mean Sample Size = 10.000.

The Post-Hoc test presents the result of the comparison between all the possible pairs. Since we have three groups, a total of six pairs will be possible in which three will be mirror images (1–2 and 2–1, 1–3 and 3–1, 2–3 and 3–2). The results are shown in three rows. The *p*-value for city 1- city 2 and city 2- city 3 comparison is shown as 0.000, whereas it is 0.284 for city 1- city 3 comparison. This means that the average sales of gasoline between city 1 and city 2 as well as city 2 and city 3 are significantly different, whereas the same is not significantly different between city 1 and city 3.

The same result is also shown in another form in the table labeled *Homogeneous Subsets*. In this table, the groups are arranged in the increasing order by the mean value. City 2 having the smallest mean value of gasoline sale is listed first followed by city 1 and city 3. On the right-hand side, the groups are clubbed in homogenous subsets. City 2 with a mean of 7.725 is put under subset 1 and city 1 and 3 with means of 13.795 and 15.265 are put under subset 2. This means that city 1 and 3 do not significantly differ from each other and form a homogenous subset whereas they are different from city 2.

Performing Planned Comparisons

In this section, we will demonstrate planned comparisons for H_{02} and H_{03} of example 5.1. In the case of *Univariate GLM*, SPSS allows us to choose from a list of preset contrasts. However, in the case of *One-Way ANOVA*, the contrasts have to be specified as will be explained later. First we explain the specifying contrasts in *Univariate GLM*. Click on *Contrasts* in the main dialogue box as shown in Figure 5.2. The resulting dialogue box is shown in Figure 5.10.

Click on the drop down arrow opposite *Contrasts* in Figure 5.10 to view the list of contrasts available. In this case, there are a total of six preset contrasts available: *Deviation, Simple, Difference, Helmert, Repeated* and *Polynomial*. If you select any of these and right click the mouse on it, SPSS *Help* will show the description of the particular command. For example, we get the following description on selecting *Deviation* and right clicking on it:

"Compares the effect of each category of the predictor variable or factor, except one, to the overall effect. Select either First or Last as the omitted category."

Figure 5.10

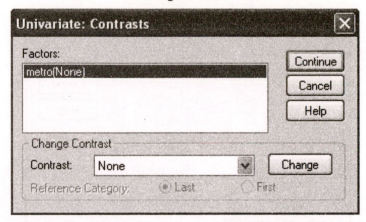

In our example, by selecting *Deviation*, we can perform two comparisons. If we select metro 1 (first) to be omitted, then the average gasoline sale for metro 2 and 3 will be compared with the overall average (gasoline sale in metro 1, 2 and 3 together). If we select metro 3 (first) to be omitted, then the average gasoline sale for metro 1 and 2 will be compared with the overall average. The other preset contrasts also have similar explanations.

In the case of *One-Way ANOVA*, clicking on *Contrasts* on the main dialogue box (Figure 5.1) opens a dialogue box as shown in Figure 5.11. Earlier, in the section on Multiple Comparisons, we explained that contrast coefficients for testing H_{02} and H_{03} are $-1, 1, 0$ and $2, -1, -1$. To specify these coefficients, type them in the *Coefficients* box and click on the *Add* button. This will transfer the coefficients to the bigger box. The coefficients should be entered one at a time with the coefficient of the lowest numbered group entering first. Click on *Next* to enter another set of coefficients. The phrase *"Contrast 1 of 1"* will get converted to *"Contrast 2 of 2"* and the boxes will become empty. Enter $2, -1$ and -1 for testing the second hypothesis. Steps for entering these two sets of coefficients are given below for clarity:

Enter -1 in the box labeled *Coefficients*
Click on the *Add* button
Enter 1 in the box labeled *Coefficients*
Click on the *Add* button

Figure 5.11

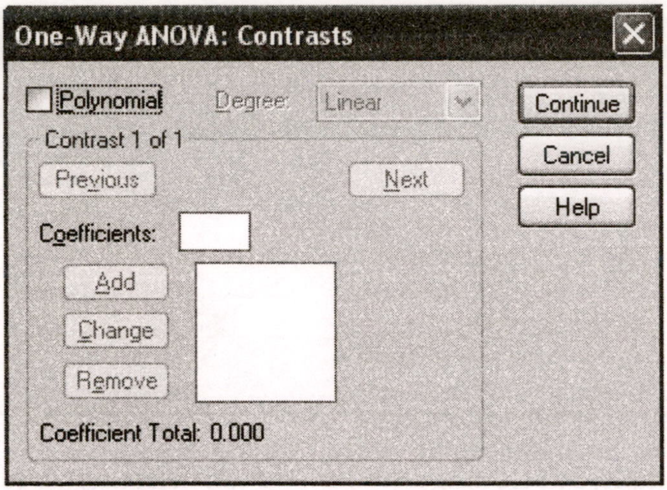

Enter 0 in the box labeled *Coefficients*
Click on the *Add* button

Coefficients for first contrast entered. Now click on the *Next* button.

Enter 2 in the box labeled *Coefficients*
Click on the *Add* button
Enter –1 in the box labeled *Coefficients*
Click on the *Add* button
Enter –1 in the box labeled *Coefficients*
Click on the *Add* button

This completes the process for entering both sets of contrast coefficients. Now click on *Continue* to return to the main dialogue box and click on *OK* to run the analysis.

Figure 5.12 presents the specific part of the output related to contrasts. The output first shows the contrast coefficients assigned by us, followed by the results of the significance test for each contrast. Two sets of results are given for each contrast, assuming variances to be equal and unequal. The result with the assumption of equal variances is the one more commonly used as unequal variance violates the ANOVA assumption.

Figure 5.12

Contrast Coefficients

	metro		
Contrast	1	2	3
1	-1	1	0
2	2	-1	-1

Contrast Tests

		Contrast	Value of Contrast	Std. Error	t	df	Sig. (2-tailed)
volume	Assume equal variances	1	-6.0700	.94841	-6.400	27	.000
		2	4.6000	1.64269	2.800	27	.009
	Does not assume equal variances	1	-6.0700	.72479	-8.375	17.167	.000
		2	4.6000	1.40129	3.283	23.889	.003

The first contrast tests if the average sale in metro 1 is the same as that in metro 2. The test result shows that the t statistic is –6.400 with 27 degrees of freedom. The corresponding two-tailed p-value is less than 0.0005. Therefore, we can reject the null hypothesis and conclude that there is significant difference in the average sale of gasoline in metro 1 and 2.

The second contrast tests if the average sale in metro 1 is same as the mean of the average sale in metro 2 and 3. The test result shows that the t-statistic is 2.800 with 27 degrees of freedom. The corresponding two-tailed p-value is less than 0.009. Therefore, we can reject this null hypothesis also.

5.2.3 Two-Way Between-Groups ANOVA

In two-way analysis, we have two independent variables or factors and we are interested in knowing their effect on the same dependent variable. The following example illustrates how this analysis can be performed.

Example 5.2

An MBA aspirant was interested in knowing the impact of educational background (arts/commerce and science/engineering) on the final placement salaries. He is also aware that previous work experience has an impact on the salaries. Therefore, he chooses educational background and work experience as two independent variables. Based on educational background, respondents are categorized into two groups—one belonging to the arts and commerce stream and the other belonging to the science and engineering stream. Based on previous work experience, respondents are again categorized into two groups—one with experience and the other without experience. Since we have two levels of each of the factors, this is called a 2*2 design. A sample of 30 students is randomly chosen and their salaries from campus recruitment as well as information on educational background and work experience are given in the Table 5.2. For educational background, 1 represents arts and commerce and 2 represents the science and engineering stream. For work experience, 1 represents students with experience and 2 represents students without experience. Salary is given in the multiple of 100,000 INR.

Table 5.2

Students	Educational Background	Work Experience	Salary	Students	Educational Background	Work Experience	Salary
1	1	1	8.50	16	2	1	9.80
2	1	1	10.80	17	2	1	10.20
3	1	1	9.70	18	2	1	11.00
4	1	1	8.80	19	2	2	7.80
5	1	2	7.80	20	2	2	7.30
6	1	1	7.50	21	2	1	6.90
7	1	1	7.80	22	2	1	6.10
8	1	1	6.90	23	2	1	6.25
9	1	2	4.50	24	2	2	3.80
10	1	2	4.10	25	2	2	3.20
11	1	1	7.70	26	2	2	5.10
12	1	2	5.50	27	2	2	4.90
13	1	2	5.60	28	2	2	4.65
14	1	2	5.20	29	2	2	4.80
15	1	2	4.10	30	2	1	5.24

The null hypothesis in this case can be stated as:

H_0: The educational background and previous work experience have no bearing on the placement salaries of MBA students.

The corresponding alternate hypothesis could be that the MBA students from science stream and/or with previous work experience will get more salaries during final placements.

The variables are labeled as *students, eduback, workexp* and *salary*. Click on *Analyze*, which will produce a drop down menu, choose *General Linear Model* from that and click on *Univariate*. The resulting dialogue box is shown in Figure 5.13.

Figure 5.13

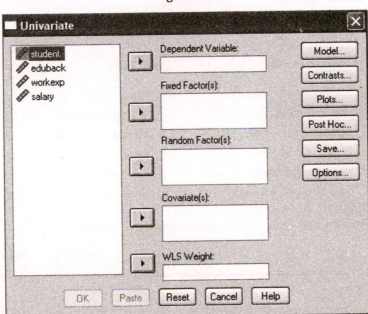

Transfer the dependent variable (salary) into the *Dependent variable* box and the independent or factor variables (eduback and workexp) into the *Fixed Factor(s)* box. Click on *Options* to ask for additional statistics. The dialogue box obtained by clicking on *Options* is shown in Figure 5.14.

Select the variables for which you want descriptive statistics from the left-hand side box labeled *Factor(s) and Factor Interactions* to the right-hand side box labeled *Display Means for*. By selecting the interaction, one can get the mean of the dependent variable for different combinations of the independent variables. Click on *Continue* to return to the mail dialogue box and click on *OK* to run the analysis.

Figure 5.14

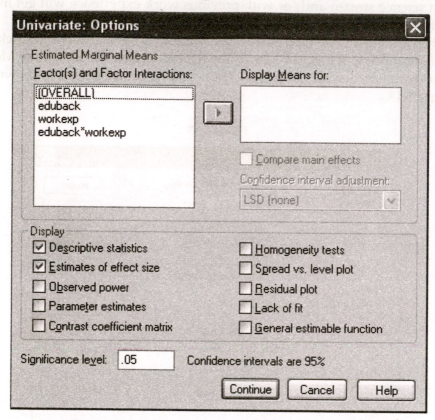

Please note that selecting *Post-Hoc* tests will not produce any results in this case as there are only two levels of each factor. A significant *F*-statistic itself tells that one group is significantly different from the other. Post-Hoc tests are meaningful if there are more than two levels of at least one of the independent variables.

Output for Two-Way ANOVA (Univariate GLM)
The output is shown in Figure 5.15. The first table labeled *Between-Subjects Factors* gives the number of subjects in each level of the factor. In this case, we have 15 students belonging to each level of the two factors. The second table labeled *Descriptive Statistics* gives us the mean, standard deviation and number of cases for the combination of different levels of the factors.

In this case, from the first row of the *Descriptive Statistics* table, we can find that the mean salary of students with work experience and from arts or commerce backgrounds is 8.46 lakhs i.e., Rs 846,000.

Figure 5.15

Univariate Analysis of Variance

Between-Subjects Factors

		N
eduback	1	15
	2	15
workexp	1	15
	2	15

Descriptive Statistics

Dependent Variable: salary

eduback	workexp	Mean	Std. Deviation	N
1	1	8.4625	1.28167	8
	2	5.2571	1.28434	7
	Total	6.9667	2.06594	15
2	1	7.9271	2.32891	7
	2	5.1938	1.58980	8
	Total	6.4693	2.36233	15
Total	1	8.2127	1.79507	15
	2	5.2233	1.40419	15
	Total	6.7180	2.19511	30

Tests of Between-Subjects Effects

Dependent Variable: salary

Source	Type III Sum of Squares	df	Mean Square	F	Sig.	Partial Eta Squared
Corrected Model	68.106[a]	3	22.702	8.240	.001	.487
Intercept	1344.773	1	1344.773	488.114	.000	.949
eduback	.669	1	.669	.243	.626	.009
workexp	65.835	1	65.835	23.896	.000	.479
eduback * workexp	.416	1	.416	.151	.701	.006
Error	71.631	26	2.755			
Total	1493.683	30				
Corrected Total	139.737	29				

a. R Squared = .487 (Adjusted R Squared = .428)

The third table labeled *Tests of Between-Subjects Effects* gives the ANOVA results. The explanation for various columns is same as given earlier in case of *One-Way ANOVA*.

We can see that the F-statistic corresponding to work experience is 23.896, which is significant at $p < .001$. F-statistic for educational background is 0.243, which is insignificant as $p = .626$. The interaction between work experience and educational background is also insignificant. Therefore the null hypothesis (H_0) is only partially supported. While the previous work experience has a significant impact on the placement salaries of MBA students, their previous educational background does not.

The results will be reported as:

"Previous work experience has a significant effect on the placement salaries of MBA students, F (1, 26) = 23.896, p < .001. However, previous education background does not affect the final placement salaries significantly, F (1, 26) = 0.243, p = .626. The interaction of previous work experience and educational background also does not affect the placement salaries significantly, F (1, 26) = 0.151, p = .701."

SYNTAX

The syntax for obtaining the above output is given below:

```
UNIANOVA
salary BY workexp eduback
/METHOD = SSTYPE(3)
/INTERCEPT = INCLUDE
/EMMEANS = TABLES(workexp)
/EMMEANS = TABLES(eduback)
/EMMEANS = TABLES(workexp*eduback)
/PRINT = DESCRIPTIVE ETASQ
/CRITERIA = ALPHA(.05)
/DESIGN = workexp eduback workexp*eduback.
```

6

Chi-Square Test of Independence for Discrete Data

Chi Square (χ^2) is one of the very popular methods for testing hypotheses on discrete data. As explained in Chapter 1, on basic statistical concepts, discrete data can be nominal or ordinal. Finding descriptive statistics for such data is meaningless. The only summary statistics useful for such data are frequencies and percentages. Contingency tables along with some chi-square statistics are used on such kind of data. Given below are some examples of business and social sciences related studies where the chi-square test of independence can be used along with contingency tables to get a meaningful insight into the problem:

- An international business researcher wants to establish if the performance (categorized as loss, breakeven and profit) of a firm is dependent on which country (categorized as low, middle and high income) it is located in.
- An organizations' researcher wants to determine if the satisfaction level (on a scale from 1 to 3) of the employees of a firm is dependent on their placement (local or international) within a firm.
- A social researcher wants to establish if the attitude towards premarital sex is dependent on the gender of the respondent.

6.1 BASIC CONCEPTS

There are three different types of chi-square analysis:

1) Chi-square test for goodness of fit,
2) Chi-square test for homogeneity,
3) Chi-square test of independence.

The chi-square test for goodness of fit determines if the sample under investigation has been drawn from a population, which follows some specified distribution, while the test for homogeneity investigates the issue whether several populations are homogeneous with respect to a particular characteristic. These two are not very common methods employed in business research and will not be dealt with here.

6.1.1 Chi-Square Test of Independence

The chi-square test of independence is used to test the hypothesis that two categorical variables are independent of each other. A small chi-square statistic indicates that the null hypothesis is correct and that the two variables are independent of each other.

The procedure involves comparing the observed cell frequencies with the expected cell frequencies. Observed cell frequencies are the actual number of cases falling in different cells of the contingency table and expected frequencies are the number of cases that should fall in each cell if there is no relationship between the two categorical variables. The basis of the test is difference between the observed frequency and the expected frequency of each cell of the contingency table. While observed cell frequencies can be directly obtained from the data given, the expected cell frequencies are calculated by multiplying the total of the row by the total of the column to which the cell belongs and then dividing by the total sample size.

Along with the chi-square statistic, we also need to find the degrees of freedom associated with the contingency table to find the significance of the relationship. Degrees of freedom is calculated by multiplying the number of rows minus one by the number of columns minus one. The degrees of freedom and significance level are used to find the values of chi-square from the standard tables. If the tabulated chi-square value is less than the calculated chi-square value, the null hypothesis is rejected and we conclude that there is some significant association between the two variables.

The test can also be applied to ordinal categorical variables. While we can test the independence of relationship between only two variables at a time, the variables themselves can have any number of levels.

6.1.2 Contingency Tables

It is often useful to look at contingency tables along with the results of the chi-square test to gain useful insight into the data. Contingency tables present the data in R X C tables where R is the number of rows and C is the number of columns. If the row variable has 3 categories and column variable has 2 categories, then the contingency table produced will be a 3X2 table. The use of the contingency table has been elaborated in more detail through the example in this chapter.

6.2 USING SPSS

Solved Example

A researcher was interested in knowing whether the performance of firms belonging to the automobile sector is independent of the location of the firm. She developed a measure of performance on a nominal scale from 1 to 3–1 representing loss, 2 breakeven and 3 profit. The location of the firm was put in one of the two categories—1 representing low- and middle-income countries and 2 representing high-income countries. The data on these two variables, collected for 45 corporations for a particular year is presented in Table 6.1.

Table 6.1

Firm	Location	Performance	Firm	Location	Performance	Firm	Location	Performance
1	1	1	16	1	3	31	2	2
2	1	1	17	1	3	32	2	2
3	1	1	18	1	3	33	2	2
4	1	1	19	1	3	34	2	2
5	1	1	20	1	3	35	2	2
6	1	1	21	1	3	36	2	2
7	1	2	22	1	3	37	2	3
8	1	2	23	1	3	38	2	3
9	1	2	24	2	1	39	2	3
10	1	2	25	2	1	40	2	3
11	1	2	26	2	1	41	2	3
12	1	3	27	2	1	42	2	3
13	1	3	28	2	1	43	2	3
14	1	3	29	2	2	44	2	3
15	1	3	30	2	2	45	2	3

The null hypothesis in this case is that performance of the firm is independent of its location. In other words, there is no significant difference in the performance of the firms located at different places.

The given data is entered in the data editor. Click on *Analyze*, which will produce a drop down menu, choose *Descriptive Statistics* and then click on *Crosstabs* as shown in Figure 6.1. The resulting dialogue box is shown in Figure 6.2.

Figure 6.1

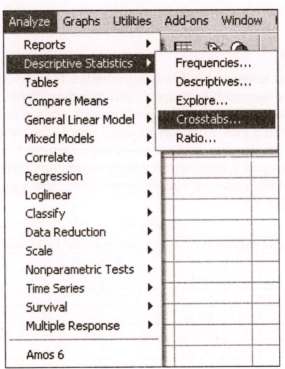

Select the variable you want to create the row of your contingency table and transfer it to the box labeled *Row(s)*, transfer the other variable to the box labeled *Column(s)*. By choosing which variable to transfer to these two boxes, you may choose the way you want the contingency table to appear. In this example we transfer *Location* to the box labeled *Row(s)* and *Performance* to the box labeled *Column(s)*. Next, click on the *Statistics* button which brings up a dialogue box as shown in Figure 6.3.

Figure 6.2

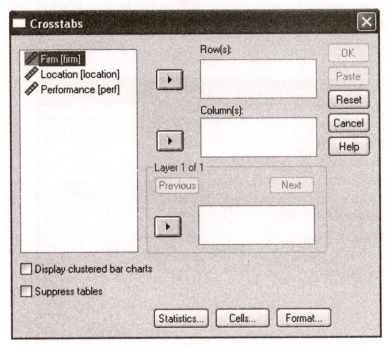

Figure 6.3

Select the first box labeled *Chi-square* and click on the *Continue* button to return to the previous screen. Now click on the button labeled *Cells* which brings up a dialogue box as shown in Figure 6.4.

Figure 6.4

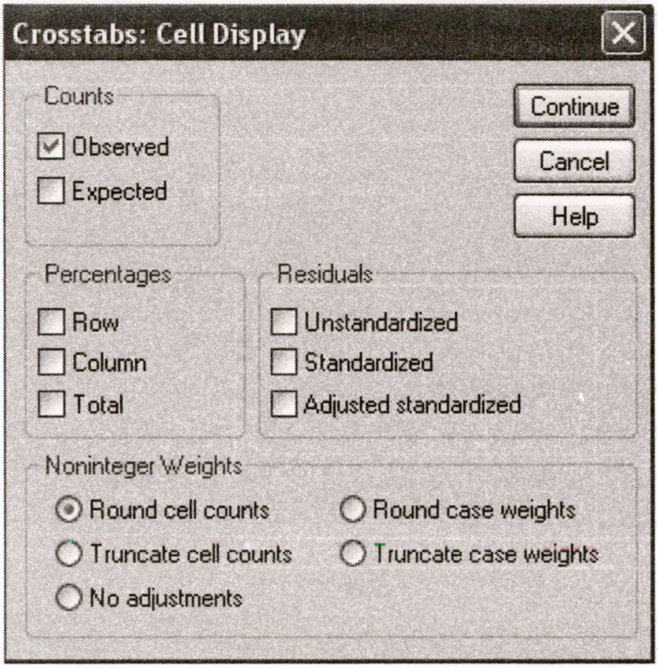

Select the values you want to produce in your output. In this example we have selected observed and expected counts. Readers may try other options. Click on *Continue* to return to the main dialogue box (Figure 6.2). The button labeled *Format* can be used to arrange the output in ascending or descending order. Click on *OK* to run the analysis.

Output

The output for *Crosstabs* is shown in Figure 6.5.

The first box labeled *Case Processing Summary* gives some details about the cases in the data file. The second box labeled *Location*Performance Crosstabulation* gives the descriptive statistics requested in the analysis. In

Figure 6.5

Crosstabs

Case Processing Summary

	Cases					
	Valid		Missing		Total	
	N	Percent	N	Percent	N	Percent
Location * Performance	45	100.0%	0	.0%	45	100.0%

Location * Performance Crosstabulation

			Performance			Total
			1	2	3	
Location	1	Count	6	5	12	23
		Expected Count	5.6	6.6	10.7	23.0
	2	Count	5	8	9	22
		Expected Count	5.4	6.4	10.3	22.0
Total		Count	11	13	21	45
		Expected Count	11.0	13.0	21.0	45.0

Chi-Square Tests

	Value	df	Asymp. Sig. (2-sided)
Pearson Chi-Square	1.190[a]	2	.552
Likelihood Ratio	1.197	2	.550
Linear-by-Linear Association	.104	1	.747
N of Valid Cases	45		

a. 0 cells (.0%) have expected count less than 5. The minimum expected count is 5.38.

this example, we requested for actual and expected count, which is produced for each location (in rows) and each performance category (in columns). *Count* tells the actual frequency falling into a particular cell. *Expected count* gives the expected frequency for each cell assuming no association. The values on each row give information for each level of the column variable whereas the values on each column give information about each level of the row variable. A chi-square test is not suitable if there are less than 5 cases in any of the cells.

The last box labeled *Chi-Square Tests* gives the results of the chi-square test. Several statistics are reported here but the one most commonly used is the *Pearson Chi-Square.* We reject the null hypothesis if 2-sided significance reported in the last column and in the row corresponding to the *Pearson Chi-Square* is less than the significance level selected (5% or 10%).

In our example the *p*-value of .552 is much higher than the commonly accepted levels of either .05 or .10. So we cannot reject the null hypothesis. In other words, there is no significant relation between the performance of a firm and its location. The result is reported as given below:

"There was no significant relationship at 10% significance level between performance of a firm and its location ($\chi^2 = 1.190$, df = 2, p = .552)."

SYNTAX

The syntax for obtaining the above output is given below (*loc* and *perf* are the variable names used for *location* and *performance* respectively):

```
CROSSTABS
/TABLES=loc BY perf
/FORMAT= AVALUE TABLES
/STATISTIC=CHISQ
/CELLS= COUNT EXPECTED .
```

7

Correlation Analysis

Correlation is a measure of relationship between two variables. It has wide application in business and statistics. Given below are some common applications of correlation analysis in business and social sciences:

- *Marketing:* The marketing manager wants to know if price reduction has any impact on increasing sales.
- *Production:* The production department wants to know if the number of defective items produced has anything to do with the age of the machine.
- *Human Resource:* The HR department wants to know if the productivity of its workers decreases with the number of hours they put in.
- *Social Sciences:* A social activist wants to know if increasing female literacy has any impact in increasing the age of marriage of the girl child.
- *Research:* An educationist wants to know if enforcing stricter attendance rules helps students in performing better in their studies.

7.1 BASIC CONCEPTS

7.1.1 Correlation Coefficient

The correlation coefficient gives a mathematical value for measuring the strength of the linear relationship between two variables. It can take values from −1 to 1 with:

(a) +1 representing absolute positive linear relationship (as X increases, Y increases).

(b) 0 representing no linear relationship (X and Y have no pattern).

(c) –1 representing absolute inverse relationship (as X increases, Y decreases).

In the SPSS program, you have an option to choose from three types of correlation coefficients: Pearson's, Kendall's tau-b and Spearman's. While Pearson's coefficient is commonly used for continuous data, the other two are used mainly for ranked data.

7.1.2 Nature of Variables

Originally correlation analysis was conceptualized for use when the two variables between which correlation is to be established, are equal interval or ratio scaled in their level of measurement, such as age, weight etc. Technically correlation analysis can be run with any kind of data, but the output will be of no use if a correlation is run on a categorical variable with more than two categories. For example, in a data set, if the respondents are categorized according to nationalities and religions, correlation between these variables is meaningless.

7.1.3 Bivariate/Partial Correlation

Bivariate correlation tests the strength of the relationship between two variables without giving any consideration to the interference some other variable might cause to the relationship between the two variables being tested. For example, while testing the correlation between the academic performance and attendance of a student, bivariate correlation will not consider the impact of some other variables like motivation level or age. In such cases, a bivariate analysis may show us a strong relationship between attendance and academic performance; but in reality, this strong relationship could be the result of some other extraneous factor like age or motivation level etc. In such cases a partial correlation should be used. It allows us to examine the correlation between two variables while czontrolling for the effects of one or more of the additional variables without throwing out any of the data.

7.2 USING SPSS

Example 7.1

There is always a hot debate in business schools during placement week that the final placements, in general, are arbitrary and a candidate's abilities do not really have any correlation with the salary package offered to her. To test the correctness of the above assumption, a sample of 30 students was randomly selected from a MBA class of a top business school. Their marks were taken as a measure of their academic performance. They were given standard tests to assess them on three other parameters, communication ability, general awareness and IQ level. After the placement week, data regarding salary was collected. The data is given in Table 7.1.

Table 7.1

Student	Salary (Lacs p.a.)	Marks (Percentage)	Communication Score	General Awareness Score	IQ Score
1	5.50	65	88	78	105
2	16.50	90	93	95	120
3	4.50	65	63	56	100
4	7.00	68	79	66	100
5	3.50	67	58	77	100
6	6.00	62	85	87	110
7	4.00	84	77	44	105
8	7.50	82	78	66	105
9	2.75	75	53	68	100
10	10.50	81	95	54	115
11	5.00	74	68	50	110
12	9.00	88	78	78	115
13	4.00	65	63	45	100
14	4.50	84	68	56	100
15	2.50	68	58	43	95
16	8.50	71	89	68	110
17	12.50	92	91	76	120
18	3.00	53	55	71	100
19	8.75	77	77	77	100

(Table 7.1 Contd.)

(Table 7.1 Contd.)

Student	Salary (Lacs p.a.)	Marks (Percentage)	Communication Score	General Awareness Score	IQ Score
20	6.50	68	79	45	105
21	13.50	89	89	56	115
22	5.50	68	64	43	100
23	4.00	63	62	40	100
24	5.00	65	69	55	100
25	7.60	74	71	68	105

Here we want to test the validity of the assumption that there is no correlation between the given variables. We also want to calculate the bivariate and partial correlation coefficients for the variables.

The data is entered in the data editor and the variables are labeled as *student, salary, marks, communic, genawar,* and *iq* respectively. Click on *Analyze,* which will produce a drop down menu as shown in Figure 7.1, choose *Correlate*. There are three types of correlation exercises shown under *Correlate—Bivariate, Partial,* and *Distances*. We will explain the computation procedure for bivariate and partial correlation here.

Figure 7.1

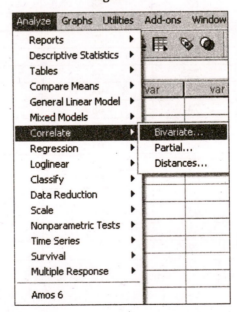

7.2.1 Bivariate Correlation

To obtain bivariate correlations click on *Bivariate* as shown in Figure 7.1. The resulting dialogue box is shown in Figure 7.2.

Choose the variables for which the correlation is to be studied from the left-hand side box and move them to the right-hand side box labeled *Variables*. Once any two variables are transferred to the variables box, the *OK* button becomes active. We will transfer all the variables other than *Student No* to the right-hand side box. There are some default selections at the bottom of the window; these can be changed by clicking on the appropriate boxes. For our purpose, we will use the most commonly used Pearson's coefficient.

Next, while choosing between one-tailed and two-tailed test of significance, we have to see if we are making any directional prediction as explained in section 2.4.3 in Chapter 2. The one-tailed test is appropriate if we are making predictions about a positive or negative relationship between the variables; however, the two-tailed test should be used if there is no prediction about the direction of relation between the variables to be tested. Finally *Flag significant correlations* asks SPSS to print an asterisk next to each correlation that is significant at the 0.05 significance level and two asterisks next to each correlation that is significant at the 0.01 significance level,

Figure 7.2

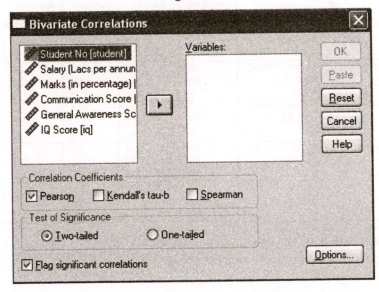

so that the output can be read easily. The default selections will serve the purpose for the problem at hand. We may choose means and standard deviations from the *Options* button if we wish to compute these figures for the given data. After making appropriate selections, click on *OK* to run the analysis.

Output

The output produced is shown in Figure 7.3. The output gives correlations for all the pairs of variables and each correlation is produced twice in the matrix. We get the following 10 correlations for the given example:

1. Salary and academic performance (marks)
2. Salary and communication abilities
3. Salary and general awareness
4. Salary and IQ level
5. Academic performance (marks) and communication abilities
6. Academic performance (marks) and general awareness

Figure 7.3

Correlations

		Salary (Lacs per annum)	Marks (in percentage)	Communication Score	General Awareness Score	IQ Score
Salary (Lacs per annum)	Pearson Correlation	1	.702**	.813**	.461*	.844**
	Sig. (2-tailed)		.000	.000	.020	.000
	N	25	25	25	25	25
Marks (in percentage)	Pearson Correlation	.702**	1	.544**	.204	.676**
	Sig. (2-tailed)	.000		.005	.328	.000
	N	25	25	25	25	25
Communication Score	Pearson Correlation	.813**	.544**	1	.389	.798**
	Sig. (2-tailed)	.000	.005		.055	.000
	N	25	25	25	25	25
General Awareness Score	Pearson Correlation	.461*	.204	.389	1	.444*
	Sig. (2-tailed)	.020	.328	.055		.026
	N	25	25	25	25	25
IQ Score	Pearson Correlation	.844**	.676**	.798**	.444*	1
	Sig. (2-tailed)	.000	.000	.000	.026	
	N	25	25	25	25	25

**. Correlation is significant at the 0.01 level (2-tailed).

*. Correlation is significant at the 0.05 level (2-tailed).

7. Academic performance (marks) and IQ level
8. Communication abilities and general awareness
9. Communication abilities and IQ level
10. General awareness and IQ level

In each cell of the correlation matrix, we get Pearson's correlation coefficient, *p*-value for two-tailed test of significance and the sample size. From the output, we can see that the correlation coefficient between salary and marks is 0.702 and the *p*-value for two-tailed test of significance is less than 0.0005 (values less than 0.0005 are shown as 0.000 in SPSS outputs). From these figures we can conclude that there is a strong positive correlation between *Salary* and *Marks* and that this correlation is significant at the significance level of 0.01. Results for correlations between other set of variables can also be interpreted similarly. We can see that *General Awareness Score* and *Marks* are not significantly correlated ($r = 0.204$, $p = 0.328$). All other variables are significantly correlated with each other.

SYNTAX

The syntax for obtaining the above output is given below:

```
CORRELATIONS
/VARIABLES=salary marks comunic genawar iq
/PRINT=TWOTAIL NOSIG
/MISSING=PAIRWISE .
```

7.2.2 Partial Correlation

To obtain partial correlations, click on *Partial* as shown in Figure 7.1. The resulting dialogue box is shown in Figure 7.4.

In partial correlation, we are interested in knowing the extent of the specific relationship between two variables, factoring out the effect of one or more other variables. For the given example, we want to find the correlation between salary and marks while controlling for the effect of the IQ level. We will transfer *Salary* and *Marks* to the *Variables* box and *IQ Score* to the *Controlling for* box. The resulting dialogue box is shown in Figure 7.5. Now click on *OK* to run the analysis.

Figure 7.4

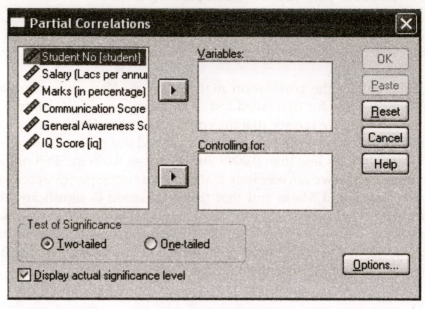

Figure 7.5

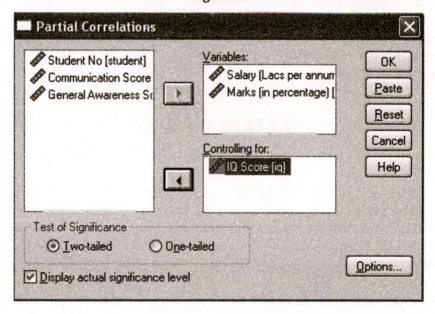

Output

The output produced is shown in Figure 7.6. The variable we are controlling for in the analysis (For example, IQ in our case) is shown in the left-hand side. We can see that the correlation coefficient is not just considerably smaller (0.333 as compared to 0.702 in case of bivariate), but the *p*-value is also much higher (0.112 as compared to less than 0.005 in case of bivariate). This means that if we control for the IQ level of the students, the salaries will not be significantly related to the academic performance of the students, which is good news indeed for happy-go-lucky students!

Figure 7.6

Partial Corr

Correlations

Control Variables			Salary (Lacs per annum)	Marks (in percentage)
IQ Score	Salary (Lacs per annum)	Correlation	1.000	.333
		Significance (2-tailed)	.	.112
		df	0	22
	Marks (in percentage)	Correlation	.333	1.000
		Significance (2-tailed)	.112	.
		df	22	0

SYNTAX

The syntax for obtaining the above output is given below:

```
PARTIAL CORR
/VARIABLES= salary marks BY iq
/SIGNIFICANCE=TWOTAIL
/MISSING=LISTWISE .
```

8

Multiple Regression

Regression analysis is used to assess the relationship between one dependent variable (DV) and several independent variables (IVs). This is the most commonly used technique in much of the social sciences research. Given below are some common applications of regression analysis in business and social sciences:

- *Marketing:* The marketing manager wants to know if sales is dependent on factors such as advertising spend, number of products introduced, number of sales personnel etc.
- *Human Resource:* The HR department wants to predict the efficiency of management trainees based on their academic performance, leadership abilities, IQ level etc.
- *Social Sciences:* A social researcher wants to predict the age of marriage of a girl based on characteristics such as her education level, parent's education level, number of siblings, and parent's annual income.

8.1 BASIC CONCEPTS

8.1.1 Regression Coefficient

Regression coefficient is a measure of how strongly each IV (also known as predictor variable) predicts the DV. There are two types of regression coefficients—unstandardized coefficients and standardized coefficients, also known as beta value. The unstandardized coefficients can be used in the equation as coefficients of different IVs along with the constant term to predict the value of DV. The standardized coefficient (beta) is, however, measured in standard deviations. A beta value of 2 associated with a particular IV indicates that a change of 1 standard deviation in that particular IV will result in a change of 2 standard deviations in the DV.

If there is just one IV to predict one DV, the beta value obtained would be same as the correlation coefficient between the DV and the IV.

8.1.2 R Values

R represents the correlation between the observed values and the predicted values (based on the regression equation obtained) of the DV. R Square is the square of R and gives the proportion of variance in the dependent variable accounted for by the set of IVs chosen for the model. R Square is used to find out how well the IVs are able to predict the DV. However, the R Square value tends to be a bit inflated when the number of IVs is more or when the number of cases is large. The adjusted R Square takes into account these things and gives more accurate information about the fitness of the model. For example, an adjusted R Square value of 0.70 would mean that the IVs in the model can predict 70% of the variance in the DV. While in natural science research it is not uncommon to get R Square values as high as 0.99, a much lower value (0.10–0.20) of R Square is acceptable in social science research.

8.1.3 Design Issues

There are a number of design issues in regression analysis and readers are suggested to consult a standard statistics textbook for details. We discuss here two important aspects of design issues—Ratio of cases to IVs and Multicollinearity.

Case to IVs ratio should be substantial for a meaningful regression solution. The rule of the thumb is to have the sample size at least as much as 50 + 8n for testing the multiple correlation and 104 + n for testing individual predictors, where n is the number of IVs.

Multicollinearity refers to a situation when two or more IVs are highly correlated with each other. Multicollinearity causes an inflation in the standard error of regression coefficients resulting in a reduction of their significance. Care should be taken in choosing the IVs such that they are not highly correlated with each other. SPSS gives diagnostic statistics for multicol-linearity which are explained later in this chapter.

8.1.4 Multiple Regression Types

There are three major types of multiple regression: standard multiple regression, hierarchical or sequential regression and stepwise or statistical regression.

In *standard multiple regression*, all the IVs are entered into the equation together. In *hierarchical regression*, IVs are entered in a pre-specified manner by the researcher, which is driven by theoretical considerations. In *stepwise regression*, order of entry of variable is solely based on statistical criteria. This is, however, a controversial procedure and hardly used in social science research.

8.2 USING SPSS

Example 8.1

A researcher wants to test some hypotheses regarding the relationship between size and age of a firm and its performance in a particular industry. Size was measured by the number of employees (in 100s) working in the firm, age was the number of years for which the firm has been operating, and performance was measured by return on equity. A sample of 50 firms was selected at random. Data on these variables is given in Table 8.1.

Table 8.1

Firm ID	Performance	Size	Age	Firm ID	Performance	Size	Age
1	10.24	20	40	26	0.86	19	43
2	3.84	2	41	27	32.92	4	50
3	10.45	20	43	28	4.01	8	44
4	27.42	19	25	29	24.10	6	35
5	14.80	3	29	30	13.93	9	24
6	11.42	33	7	31	2.48	65	29
7	1.90	4	30	32	8.27	4	43
8	23.51	29	57	33	2.65	8	41

(Table 8.1 Contd.)

(Table 8.1 Contd.)

Firm ID	Performance	Size	Age	Firm ID	Performance	Size	Age
9	15.52	87	15	34	13.48	7	48
10	6.40	29	48	35	3.30	28	18
11	−2.53	11	44	36	6.44	15	32
12	5.77	20	34	37	−3.89	9	32
13	−4.35	17	16	38	1.26	78	14
14	2.81	8	18	39	24.48	99	12
15	24.70	13	16	40	14.40	8	15
16	11.92	66	17	41	0.76	6	19
17	−18.75	8	40	42	2.29	1	21
18	50.32	85	16	43	26.91	4	86
19	−16.83	1	44	44	24.64	1	56
20	15.31	5	34	45	20.62	51	21
21	5.51	7	22	46	6.72	1	22
22	6.06	61	31	47	13.80	7	61
23	14.81	21	16	48	23.91	5	88
24	42.42	93	12	49	1.88	1	11
25	−3.18	2	17	50	1.79	66	25

The researcher wanted to test the following two hypotheses:

H1: Performance of a firm is positively related to its size.
H2: Performance of a firm is positively related to its age.

The null hypotheses in this case would be that performance is not related to the size or age of the firm.

8.2.1 Standard Multiple Regression

The given data is entered in the data editor and the variables are labeled as *id, perf, size* and *age*. Click on *Analyze*, which will produce a drop down menu, choose *Regression* from that and click on *Linear* as shown in Figure 8.1. The resulting dialogue box is shown in Figure 8.2.

Transfer the dependent variable into the right-hand side box labeled *Dependent*. Transfer the independent variables into the box labeled *Independent(s)*. The DV in our example is *Performance* and the IVs are *size* and *age*. Next, we

Figure 8.1

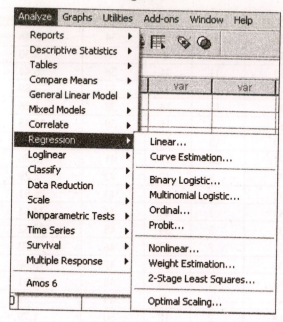

Figure 8.2

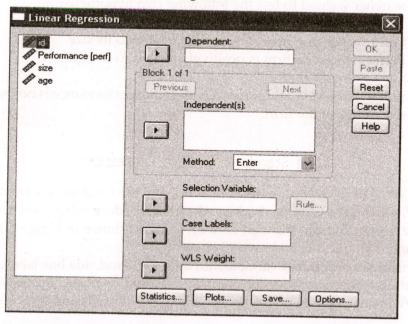

have to select the method for analysis in the box labeled *Method*. SPSS gives five options here: *Enter, Stepwise, Remove, Backward* and *Forward*. In the absence of a strong theoretical reason for using a particular method, *Enter* should be used. The box labeled *Selection Variable* is used if we want to restrict the analysis to cases satisfying particular selection criteria. The box labeled *Case Labels* is used for designating a variable to identify points on plots.

After making the appropriate selections click on the *Statistics* button. This will produce a dialogue box labeled *Linear Regression: Statistics* as shown in Figure 8.3.

Figure 8.3

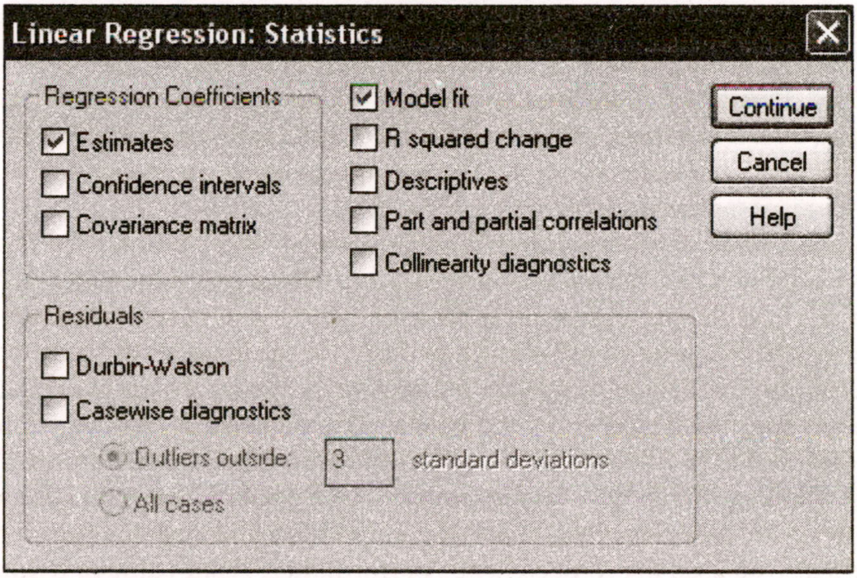

Tick against the statistics you want in the output. The *Estimates* option gives the estimate of regression coefficients.The *Model fit* option gives the fit indices for the overall model. The *Descriptives* option gives the descriptive statistics of the selected variables. The *Collinearity diagnostics* option produces important statistics used for assessing the presence of multicollinearity in the data. These four are selected in our example. Besides these, the *R squared change* option is used to get the incremental R Square value when the models change. It should be selected in the case of hierarchical regression or when we use any other method in place of *Enter* for regression strategy. Others are not commonly used. Click on the *Continue* button to return to the main dialogue box.

There are some other buttons in the main dialogue box for advanced users. The *Plots* button in the main dialogue box (Figure 8.2) may be used for producing histograms and normal probability plots of residuals. The *Save* button can be used to save statistics like predicted values, residuals and distances. The *Options* button can be used to specify the criteria for step-wise regression. Advanced users may experiment with these additional features.

Click on *OK* in the main dialogue box (Figure 8.2) to run the analysis.

Output

The output produced has several tables titled *Descriptive Statistics, Correlations, Variables Entered/Removed, Model Summary, ANOVA, Coefficients, Collinearity Diagnostics*. *Descriptive Statistics, Correlations,* and *ANOVA* tables are explained earlier in the book. The remaining tables are explained in the following paragraphs.

Figure 8.4 has two tables titled *Variables Entered/Removed* and *Model Summary*. The table titled *Variables Entered/Removed* tells us about the independent variables and the regression method used. Here we can see that both the IVs, *Age* and *Size* are entered simultaneously for the analysis as we selected the *Enter* method. The next table titled *Model Summary* gives us the R values for assessing the overall fit of the model. The adjusted R Square value in this case is 0.138. This tells us that the two IVs in our model account for 13.8% variance in the DV—performance of the firms. Clearly this is not a very good model as there are factors other than age and size of a firm which should also be used to predict a firm's performance. What value of R Square is good enough to claim that a model is good, is a judgement call of the researcher and varies for different research streams. One should look at articles in commonly used journals in one's stream to find out the acceptable R Square value for a 'good' model fit.

Figure 8.4

Variables Entered/Removed[b]

Model	Variables Entered	Variables Removed	Method
1	age, size[a]	.	Enter

a. All requested variables entered.

b. Dependent Variable: Performance

Model Summary

Model	R	R Square	Adjusted R Square	Std. Error of the Estimate
1	.416[a]	.173	.138	12.17781

a. Predictors: (Constant), age, size

Figure 8.5 has tables titled *Coefficients* and *Collinearity Diagnostics*.

Figure 8.5

Coefficients[a]

Model		Unstandardized Coefficients		Standardized Coefficients	t	Sig.	Collinearity Statistics	
		B	Std. Error	Beta			Tolerance	VIF
1	(Constant)	-.356	4.664		-.076	.939		
	size	.209	.068	.447	3.081	.003	.835	1.198
	age	.190	.107	.257	1.769	.083	.835	1.198

a. Dependent Variable: Performance

Collinearity Diagnostics[a]

Model	Dimension	Eigenvalue	Condition Index	Variance Proportions		
				(Constant)	size	age
1	1	2.311	1.000	.02	.05	.03
	2	.609	1.948	.01	.55	.09
	3	.080	5.372	.97	.40	.88

a. Dependent Variable: Performance

The first of these tables gives the regression coefficients and their significance. These regression coefficients can be used to construct an *Ordinary Least Squares (OLS)* equation and also to test the hypotheses on each of the IVs. Using the regression coefficients for IVs and the constant term given under the column labeled *B*, one can construct the OLS equation for predicting firm performance as:

$$Performance = -0.356 + (0.209)\ (Size) + (0.190)\ (Age)$$

The values given under the column labeled *Beta* can also be used to construct the regression equation if all IVs were first converted to Z scores. A variable can be converted to Z score by first subtracting the mean of the variable and then dividing the resultant value by standard deviation for a particular variable and in a particular sample. This process is known as standardization of variables. If all variables are in standardized form the Y intercept (constant term) will always be zero. This is why we do not get a constant term under the *Beta* column. The OLS equation in this case will be:

$$Z_{Performance} = (0.447)\ (Z_{Size}) + (0.257)\ (Z_{Age})$$

Now we test our hypotheses. The null hypothesis is that there is no relationship, i.e., the *beta* coefficient is not different from zero. The *p*-value for beta coefficient of *Size* is 0.003, the same for *Age* is 0.083. Both these values are significant at 10% significance level. Thus we cannot accept the null hypothesis. In other words, we can claim that the performance of a firm is positively related to its size and age. Please note that at 5% significance level, the relationship between performance and age will not be significant.

The last column in the *Coefficients* table is *Collinearity Statistics*. In this column and in the last table titled *Collinearity Diagnostics*, we get statistics for testing multicollinearity in the model. *Collinearity Statistics* gives two values—*Tolerance* and *VIF* (variance inflation factor). As one can see *Tolerance* is just the inverse of *VIF*. A value of *VIF* higher than five (or *Tolerance* less than 0.2) indicates the presence of multicollinearity. In social sciences research, a VIF value as high as 10 is considered to be acceptable. The *Condition index* obtained in the table titled *Collinearity Diagnostics* is another measure of multicollinearity. The rule of thumb in this case is that there is multi-collinearity if any two IVs have *Variance Proportions* in excess of 0.9 (column values) corresponding to any row in which *Condition index* is in excess of 30. Although these diagnostic statistics are commonly used to detect multi-collinearity, there effectiveness is controversial and one should be careful about their use.

Once multicollinearity is detected in the model, the regression coefficients are likely to be meaningless. One may consider removing some IVs which are highly correlated to reduce multicollinearity. However, if theoretical considerations do not allow removing any of the IVs, one may consider another type of regression called *ridge regression*. Ridge regression is a controversial process and not available in SPSS through the point and click method. If, after consulting literature, one still wants to use it, it is available through a macro in SPSS.

SYNTAX

The syntax for obtaining the above output is given below:

```
REGRESSION
/DESCRIPTIVES MEAN STDDEV CORR SIG N
/MISSING LISTWISE
/STATISTICS COEFF OUTS R ANOVA COLLIN TOL
/CRITERIA=PIN(.05) POUT(.10)
/NOORIGIN
/DEPENDENT perf
/METHOD=ENTER size age.
```

8.2.2 Hierarchical Regression

Hierarchical regression is in many ways similar to a standard multiple regression, the only difference being in the way IVs are entered in the model. For example, in the above solved example, theoretical considerations may demand that we first assess the model with only the size of the firm and introduce the age of the firm in the second stage. This modeling procedure is called hierarchical, as we are entering the IVs based on certain rules of hierarchy. Researchers commonly use this method when they have a theoretical reason to build models in a hierarchical manner. The procedure is explained briefly for the solved example for standard multiple regression.

Follow the steps as in the case of standard multiple regression and open the dialogue box as shown in Figure 8.2. Transfer *Performance* into the box labeled *Dependent* and *size* into the box labeled *Independent(s)*. Once *size* is entered, a button labeled *Next* becomes active above this box. Clicking on *Next* will again empty the box labeled *Independent(s)*. Transfer the second IV, *age* into this box. Next, click on the *Statistics* button to open the dialogue box shown in Figure 8.3. Select *R Squared change* in this box since we are interested in finding the incremental R square when we include more IVs. Click on *OK* to run the analysis.

Output

The output produced is quite similar to the one we got in standard multiple regression. The relevant output is shown in Figures 8.6 and 8.7.

Figure 8.6

Variables Entered/Removed[b]

Model	Variables Entered	Variables Removed	Method
1	size[a]	.	Enter
2	age[a]	.	Enter

a. All requested variables entered.

b. Dependent Variable: Performance

Model Summary

Model	R	R Square	Adjusted R Square	Std. Error of the Estimate	Change Statistics				
					R Square Change	F Change	df1	df2	Sig. F Change
1	.343[a]	.118	.099	12.44516	.118	6.397	1	48	.015
2	.416[b]	.173	.138	12.17781	.055	3.131	1	47	.083

a. Predictors: (Constant), size

b. Predictors: (Constant), size, age

The first table labeled *Variables* in Figure 8.6 titled *Entered/Removed* shows that *size* was entered in Model one followed by *age* in Model two. Please note that Model one includes only *size* as IV whereas Model two includes both *size* as well as *age* as IVs.

Figure 8.7

Coefficients[a]

Model		Unstandardized Coefficients		Standardized Coefficients	t	Sig.	Collinearity Statistics	
		B	Std. Error	Beta			Tolerance	VIF
1	(Constant)	6.867	2.305		2.980	.005		
	size	.160	.063	.343	2.529	.015	1.000	1.000
2	(Constant)	-.356	4.664		-.076	.939		
	size	.209	.068	.447	3.081	.003	.835	1.198
	age	.190	.107	.257	1.769	.083	.835	1.198

a. Dependent Variable: Performance

Excluded Variables[b]

Model		Beta In	t	Sig.	Partial Correlation	Collinearity Statistics		Minimum Tolerance
						Tolerance	VIF	
1	age	.257[a]	1.769	.083	.250	.835	1.198	.835

a. Predictors in the Model: (Constant), size

b. Dependent Variable: Performance

Collinearity Diagnostics[a]

Model	Dimension	Eigenvalue	Condition Index	Variance Proportions		
				(Constant)	size	age
1	1	1.646	1.000	.18	.18	
	2	.354	2.155	.82	.82	
2	1	2.311	1.000	.02	.05	.03
	2	.609	1.948	.01	.55	.09
	3	.080	5.372	.97	.40	.88

a. Dependent Variable: Performance

The next table—*Model Summary* in the same figure shows different R values along with change statistics for both the models in different rows. In this table we get some additional statistics under the column *Change Statistics*. Under *Change Statistics*, the first column labeled *R Square Change* gives change in the value of R Square between the models. The last column labeled *Sig. F Change* tests whether there is a significant improvement in models as we introduce additional IVs. In other words it tells us if the inclusion of additional IVs in different steps helps in explaining significant additional variance in the DV. We can see that the *R Square Change* value in row two is 0.055. This means that inclusion of *age* after *size* helps in explaining the additional 5.5% variance in the *performance* of the firms. Before inclusion of *age, size* accounted for 11.8 variance (R Squared value) in performance. Please note that *R Square Change* is same as the difference in the *R Square* values between Model two and Model one. The *p*-value for testing significance of corresponding *F* change is 0.083, significant at 10% level of significance. This means that inclusion of *age* significantly improves our model to predict firm performance.

Let us take a look at Figure 8.7 now. The first table labeled *Coefficients* gives regression coefficients and related statistics for two models separately in different rows. The second table labeled *Excluded Variables* lists the variables which are not included in earlier models but included in later models. This is not of much practical importance. Explanations for rest of the items in this figure are similar to what has been given under standard multiple regression.

SYNTAX

The syntax for obtaining the above output is given below:

```
REGRESSION
/DESCRIPTIVES MEAN STDDEV CORR SIG N
/MISSING LISTWISE
/STATISTICS COEFF OUTS R ANOVA COLLIN TOL CHANGE
/CRITERIA=PIN(.05) POUT(.10)
/NOORIGIN
/DEPENDENT perf
/METHOD=ENTER size /METHOD=ENTER age.
```

9

Logistic Regression

Logistic regression is used to predict a discrete outcome based on variables which may be discrete, continuous or mixed. Thus when the dependent variable may have two or more than two discrete outcomes, logistic regression is a commonly used technique. Following are some common applications of logistic regression analysis in business and social sciences:

- *Marketing:* An international marketing manager of a big firm is interested in predicting whether foreign subsidiaries in a particular country will make profits or losses or will they just breakeven depending on the characteristics of the host country of the subsidiary's operations. The DV here is clearly discrete with three possible outcomes—loss, breakeven or profit.
- *Human Resource:* The HR manager of a company wants to predict the absenteeism pattern of its employees based on their individual characteristics. The DV here is dichotomous—absent or present.
- *Social Sciences:* A psychologist wants to predict the pattern of awakening from sleep at night based on the personal characteristics of the subjects and characteristics of the ambience. The DV is again dichotomous.

9.1 BASIC CONCEPTS

9.1.1 Logistic Regression Coefficients

Logistic regression computes the log odds for a particular outcome. The odds of an outcome are given by the ratio of the probability of it happening and not happening as $P/(1-P)$, where P is the probability of an event. There are some mathematical problems in reporting these odds, so natural logarithms (loge) of these odds are calculated. These values may vary from − infinite to + infinite. A positive value indicates that odds are in favor of the event and the event is likely to occur while a negative value indicates that odds are against the event and the event is not likely to occur.

The above discussion is important in understanding the difference in the interpretation of multiple regression coefficients and logistic regression coefficients. For example, in a simple regression involving one DV and one IV, a regression coefficient of 2 for the IV indicates that for a unit change in the value of the IV, the DV will change by 2 units. No such direct correspondence can be established in case of logistic regression. Researchers on the other hand rely on the concept of odds as explained above to interpret the results. A change in one unit on the part of an IV will multiply the odds by exp(B), where B is the logistic regression coefficient for the IV under consideration.

9.1.2 Fit Indices

Unlike multiple regression, we do not get any exact R Square values in case of logistic regression. Instead we get two approximations—*Cox & Snell R Square* and *Nagelkerke R Square*. For establishing model fit, SPSS calculates χ^2 values based on log-likelihood values. These are further explained at appropriate places in the output section.

9.1.3 Design Issues

Logistic regression is sensitive to problems of small sample size and multicollinearity etc. in a manner similar to multiple regression. Please refer to the previous chapter on multiple regression for a discussion on these.

9.1.4 Logistic Regression Types

The dependent variable in logistic regression may have two or more outcomes. If the DV has only two outcomes, the method is called *Binary Logistic Regression*. However, if there are more than two outcomes associated with the DV, the method is called *Multinomial Logistic Regression*. We will only discuss binary logistic regression, though procedure for multinomial logistic regression is pretty much the same. Like multiple regression, the model development can be in the standard manner or hierarchical manner.

In the following section we explain the hierarchical binary logistic regression procedure. Please note that building the model in a hierarchical manner should be driven by sound theoretical considerations. The hierarchy of variables specified in this example is only for illustrative purpose.

9.2 USING SPSS

Example 9.1

As in example 8.1 in the multiple regression chapter, suppose that a researcher wants to test the same hypotheses regarding the relationship between size and age of a firm and its performance in a particular industry. Size is measured by the number of employees (in 100s) working in the firm, age is the number of years for which the firm has been operating. The performance variable is, however, measured with the help of a survey in which the CEO of the firm has to mention if his firm is making profit or loss. A response of *one* indicates profit and *zero* indicates loss. A sample of 50 firms is selected at random. Data on these variables is given in Table 9.1.

Table 9.1

Firm ID	Performance	Size	Age	Firm ID	Performance	Size	Age
1	1	20	40	26	1	19	43
2	0	2	41	27	1	4	50
3	1	20	43	28	0	8	44
4	1	19	25	29	0	6	35
5	0	3	29	30	0	9	24
6	0	33	7	31	1	65	29
7	0	4	30	32	0	4	43
8	1	29	57	33	0	8	41
9	1	87	15	34	0	7	48
10	1	29	48	35	1	28	18
11	0	11	44	36	1	15	32
12	1	20	34	37	0	9	32
13	0	17	16	38	1	78	14

(Table 9.1 Contd.)

(Table 9.1 Contd.)

Firm ID	Performance	Size	Age	Firm ID	Performance	Size	Age
14	0	8	18	39	1	99	12
15	0	13	16	40	0	8	15
16	1	66	17	41	0	6	19
17	1	8	40	42	0	1	21
18	1	85	16	43	1	4	86
19	0	1	44	44	1	1	56
20	0	5	34	45	1	51	21
21	0	7	22	46	0	1	22
22	1	61	31	47	1	7	61
23	1	21	16	48	1	5	88
24	1	93	12	49	0	1	11
25	0	2	17	50	1	66	25

The researcher wants to test following two hypotheses:

H1: Performance of a firm is positively related to its size.
H2: Performance of a firm is positively related to its age.

The null hypotheses in this case would be that performance is not related to the size or age of the firm. In addition to the above, the researcher also wants to test for the interaction effect of age and size on firm performance. The interaction hypothesis is given below:

H3: Size of a firm interacts with its age in determining firm performance such that effect of size on performance increases with the age of the firms. In other words, bigger and older firms have better performance than bigger but newer firms.

While calculating hierarchical regressions, the researcher has to decide the hierarchy of the variables entering into the equation which should be theory driven. In this example, we are also testing an interaction hypothesis (H3). When testing for interaction effects, it is advisable to build models such that we enter all the main effects in one model first, and then enter interaction effects in another model. Thus the hierarchy of variables in our example will be to enter the main effects of *size* and *age* in Model one and enter the interaction effect of *size* and *age* in Model two.

The given data is entered in the data editor and the variables are labeled as *id*, *perf*, *size* and *age*. Click on *Analyze*, which will produce a drop down menu, choose *Regression* from that and click on *Binary Logistic* as shown in Figure 9.1. The resulting dialogue box is shown in Figure 9.2.

Figure 9.1

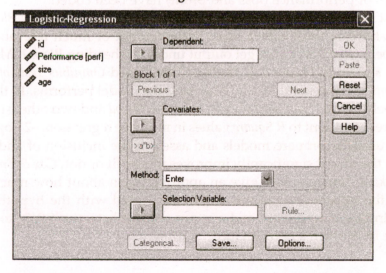

Figure 9.2

Transfer the DV (*Performance*) into the right-hand side box labeled *Dependent*. Transfer the IVs into the box labeled *Covariates*. *Size* and *age* are two IVs here. On transferring any one IV into the *Covariates* box, the button labeled *Next* becomes active. After *size* and *age* are transferred, click on the *Next* button. Now we have to enter the interaction effect in the second model. Select *size* and *age* simultaneously. Once any two variables are selected simultaneously, a button labeled >*a*∗*b*> becomes active. Click on this and the two variables will appear as *age*∗*size* in the covariates box. This essentially means that we are entering a multiplication term for age and size.

Next we have to select the method for analysis in the box labeled *Method*. SPSS gives seven options, of which *Enter* is the most commonly used. Once the DV and IVs are transferred to the relevant boxes, the button labeled *Categorical* becomes active. If any of the IVs are categorical, click on this and define the categorical variables. In this example, we do not have any categorical IVs. For common purpose one does not need to use the *Save* and *Options* buttons. Advanced users may experiment with these. Click on *OK* to run the analysis.

Output

The output is shown in Figures 9.3 to 9.5. In Figure 9.3, the first table titled *Case Processing Summary* gives the description of cases selected for analysis. The second table titled *Dependent Variable Encoding* describes how the two outcomes of performance (loss and profit) have been coded.

We get some more tables under the heading *Block 0: Beginning Block*. We are not showing these tables here. These are not of much relevance and should be ignored. Next, we get output under the heading *Block 1: Method = Enter* as shown in Figure 9.4. The first table titled *Omnibus Tests of Model Coefficients* gives general tests of how well the model performs. In the next table labeled *Model Summary* we get –2 *Log likelihood* and two other statistics which are equivalent to *R Square* values in multiple regression. –2 Log likelihood is used to compare models and assess if the inclusion of additional terms in the model significantly improves model fit or not. *Cox & Snell* and *Nagelkerke* R Square values give an approximation about how much variance in the dependent variable can be explained with the hypothesized model. In this example *age* and *size* can explain between 6.04% to 8.05% variance in the firm's performance.

Figure 9.3

Logistic Regression

Case Processing Summary

Unweighted Cases[a]		N	Percent
Selected Cases	Included in Analysis	50	100.0
	Missing Cases	0	.0
	Total	50	100.0
Unselected Cases		0	.0
Total		50	100.0

a. If weight is in effect, see classification table for the total number of cases.

Dependent Variable Encoding

Original Value	Internal Value
Loss	0
Profit	1

Next, we get the classification table, which summarizes the results of our prediction about firm performance based on size and age of a firm. We can see that our model can correctly predict 83.3% of the loss making firms and 84.6% of the profit making firms. Over all, our model predicts 84% of the firms correctly.

The last table gives Beta coefficients for the independent variables along with their significance. Positive Beta coefficients for *size* and *age* mean that with increasing *size* and *age* of a firm, its chances of having a profitable performance improve. In the column under *Sig.* we can see that *size* is significant at 0.005 level and *age* is significant at 0.01 level.

The Beta coefficients in logistic regression are not easily interpretable. For their interpretation we look at the last column under *Exp(B)*. *Exp(B)* takes a value of more than one if Beta coefficient is positive and less than 1 if it is negative. In this example, a value of 1.209 for *age* indicates that for one year increase in the *age* of the firm, the odds of a firm having a profitable performance increases by a factor of 1.209.

Figure 9.4

Block 1: Method = Enter

Omnibus Tests of Model Coefficients

		Chi-square	df	Sig.
Step 1	Step	46.268	2	.000
	Block	46.268	2	.000
	Model	46.268	2	.000

Model Summary

Step	-2 Log likelihood	Cox & Snell R Square	Nagelkerke R Square
1	22.966[a]	.604	.805

a. Estimation terminated at iteration number 8 because parameter estimates changed by less than .001.

Classification Table[a]

			Predicted		
			Performance		Percentage Correct
Observed			Loss	Profit	
Step 1	Performance	Loss	20	4	83.3
		Profit	4	22	84.6
	Overall Percentage				84.0

a. The cut value is .500

Variables in the Equation

		B	S.E.	Wald	df	Sig.	Exp(B)
Step 1[a]	size	.324	.115	7.885	1	.005	1.382
	age	.190	.074	6.613	1	.010	1.209
	Constant	-10.900	3.919	7.737	1	.005	.000

a. Variable(s) entered on step 1: size, age.

Since we built our models in a hierarchical manner, entering the interaction of age and size in model 2, we get another set of output under the heading *Block 2: Method = Enter* as shown in Figure 9.5.

Figure 9.5

Block 2: Method = Enter

Omnibus Tests of Model Coefficients

		Chi-square	df	Sig.
Step 1	Step	.385	1	.535
	Block	.385	1	.535
	Model	46.654	3	.000

Model Summary

Step	-2 Log likelihood	Cox & Snell R Square	Nagelkerke R Square
1	22.581[a]	.607	.809

a. Estimation terminated at iteration number 8 because parameter estimates changed by less than .001.

Classification Table[a]

			Predicted		
			Performance		Percentage
	Observed		Loss	Profit	Correct
Step 1	Performance	Loss	20	4	83.3
		Profit	4	22	84.6
	Overall Percentage				84.0

a. The cut value is .500

Variables in the Equation

		B	S.E.	Wald	df	Sig.	Exp(B)
Step 1[a]	size	.262	.148	3.134	1	.077	1.300
	age	.163	.085	3.725	1	.054	1.177
	age by size	.003	.004	.376	1	.540	1.003
	Constant	-10.095	4.098	6.069	1	.014	.000

a. Variable(s) entered on step 1: age * size .

Looking at the last table labeled *Variables in the Equation* in Figure 9.5, we can see that the coefficient of *Age by Size* is not significant ($p = 0.54$). This is also evident from the first table labeled *Omnibus Tests of Model Coefficients* in Figure 9.5. The incremental chi-square value is shown as 0.385 and not significant ($p = 0.535$), implying that the inclusion of an additional term in the form of interaction between *Age* and *Size* does not improve the model fit.

SYNTAX

The syntax for obtaining the above output is given below:

```
LOGISTIC REGRESSION VAR=perf
/METHOD=ENTER size age
/METHOD=ENTER age*size
/CRITERIA PIN(.05) POUT(.10) ITERATE(20) CUT(.5) .
```

10

Data Reduction and Scale Reliability: Factor Analysis

Factor analysis (FA) and Principal Components Analysis (PCA) are techniques used when the researcher is interested in identifying a smaller number of factors underlying a large number of observed variables. Variables that have a high correlation between them, and are largely independent of other subsets of variables, are combined into factors. A common usage of PCA and FA is in developing objective instruments for measuring constructs which are not directly observable in real life. The examples given below demonstrate the usage of factor analysis:

- A researcher is interested in identifying celebrity characteristics which are perceived by the general public to be important. The researcher may choose a variety of variables such as intelligence, attractiveness, dependability etc. and ask the respondents to rate their importance for a celebrity. A factor analysis of these items may reveal the underlying dimensions of important celebrity characteristics.
- A researcher collects data on many variables representing a few underlying dimensions. She then wants to have a score for each of these dimensions, which can be further used for regression or other analysis. One can obtain such scores for each of the dimension by performing a factor analysis.

10.1 BASIC CONCEPTS

10.1.1 Factor and Component

Factors are produced by FA, while components are produced by PCA. Both FA and PCA essentially are data reduction techniques. Mathematically, the difference is in the variance of the observed variables that is analyzed. In PCA, all the variance in the observed variables is analyzed whereas in FA, only shared variance is analyzed. Even though PCA is different from other techniques of FA, at many places it is treated as one of the FA techniques. For this reason, we will use the word components and factors interchangeably in this chapter.

10.1.2 Exploratory and Confirmatory Factor Analysis

As the name suggests, in exploratory FA (EFA) we are interested in exploring the underlying dimensions that could have caused correlations among the observed variables. In case of confirmatory FA (CFA), the researcher is interested in testing whether the correlations among the observed variables are consistent with the hypothesized factor structure. Thus while EFA deals with theory building, CFA deals with theory testing. The term FA generally means exploratory FA. SPSS can only do EFA analysis. For CFA, one has to use other programs such as AMOS, LISEREL, EQS etc.

10.1.3 Extraction

Extraction refers to the process of obtaining underlying factors or components. Besides PCA, SPSS offers several other extraction methods such as principal axis factoring (PAF), alpha factoring etc. The differences are primarily mathematical in nature and generate similar results in most of the cases. The two most commonly used extraction methods are PCA and PAF. If the researcher has designed the study based on a theoretical consideration, PFA should be the preferred choice. However, if the main aim of the researcher is simply to reduce the number of variables, PCA is a better choice.

10.1.4 Factor Loadings

FA produces factor loadings for each combination of extracted factors and the observed variables. Factor loadings are similar to correlation coefficients between the factors and the variables. Thus higher the factor loading, the more likely it is that the factor underlies that variable. Factor loadings help in identifying which variables are associated with the particular factors.

10.1.5 Rotation

Factor loadings obtained from extraction may not present a clear picture of the factor structure of the data set. After extraction, while we may be able to identify the number of factors, we may not know the exact way in which the observed variables load on different factors. Un-rotated factor loadings are extremely hard to interpret, regardless of the extraction methods. Rotation helps in arriving at a simple pattern of factor loadings by maximizing high correlations and minimizing low ones.

Rotation could be orthogonal or oblique. Orthogonal rotation should be used under the assumption that the underlying factors are uncorrelated with each other. However, if the researcher has theoretical reasons to believe that the factors may be correlated, oblique rotation is a better choice. SPSS offers three orthogonal rotation techniques—varimax, quartimax, and equamax; and two oblique rotation techniques—direct oblimin and promax. Of these, varimax is the most commonly used rotation technique.

10.1.6 Communalities

Communality gives the variance accounted for a particular variable by all the factors. Mathematically, it is the sum of squared loadings for a variable across all the factors. The higher the value of communality for a particular variable after extraction, higher is its amount of variance explained by the extracted factors.

10.1.7 Eigenvalue and Scree Plot

Both eigenvalue and scree plot are used to decide the number of underlying factors after extraction. Eigenvalue is the measure of amount of total variance in the data explained by a factor. Factor analysis initially considers the number of factors to be same as the total number of variables. Looking at the eigenvalue, one can determine if the factor explains sufficient amount of variance to be considered as a meaningful factor. An eigenvalue of less than one essentially means that the factor explains less variance than a single variable, and therefore should not be considered to be a meaningful factor.

Scree plot is a graphical presentation of eigenvalues of all of the factors initially considered for extraction. Usage of scree plot for deciding on the number of factors is explained later with an example.

10.1.8 Scale Reliability

After identifying the dimensions underlying a factor, a researcher may prepare a scale of those dimensions to measure the factor. Such a scale has to be tested for validity and reliability. Proper validity and reliability testing can be done using CFA. However, researchers commonly use the Cronbach alpha coefficient for establishing scale reliability. The Cronbach alpha coefficient is an indicator of internal consistency of the scale. A high value of the Cronbach alpha coefficient suggests that the items that make up the scale "hang together" and measure the same underlying construct. A value of Cronbach alpha above 0.70 can be used as a reasonable test of scale reliability.

10.1.9 Sample Size Considerations

An adequate sample size is important for identifying the correct factor structure. A sample size of less than 100 is not very suitable for conducting factor analysis. A sample size above 500 is considered to be excellent. As a rule of thumb, a sample size of 200–300 should be considered to be adequate for a proper analysis.

10.2 USING SPSS

10.2.1 Factor Analysis

Example 10.1

An advertising firm was interested in developing a scale to measure the credibility of celebrities in public opinion so that the right celebrities could be chosen for endorsing products. Based on extensive literature, they identified a list of 14 qualities, which could be important for establishing the credibility of a celebrity in public opinion. Respondents were asked to rank the credibility of some popular celebrities on a scale of 1 to 5 with respect to these qualities. The data for 56 respondents are given at the end of this chapter in Table 10.1. Please note that 56 is too small a sample size; however, it will serve our purpose of demonstrating the analysis. The 14 items measured the following characteristics:

Attractive, classy, beautiful, elegant, sexy, dependable, honest, reliable, trustworthy, sincere, expert, experienced, knowledgeable, qualified.

The given data was entered in the data editor and the items were assigned names and labels. The procedure for using the SPSS program in developing this scale is as follows: Click on *Analyze*, which will produce a drop down menu, choose *Data reduction* from the menu and click on *Factor* as shown in Figure 10.1. The resulting dialogue box is shown in Figure 10.2.

Figure 10.1

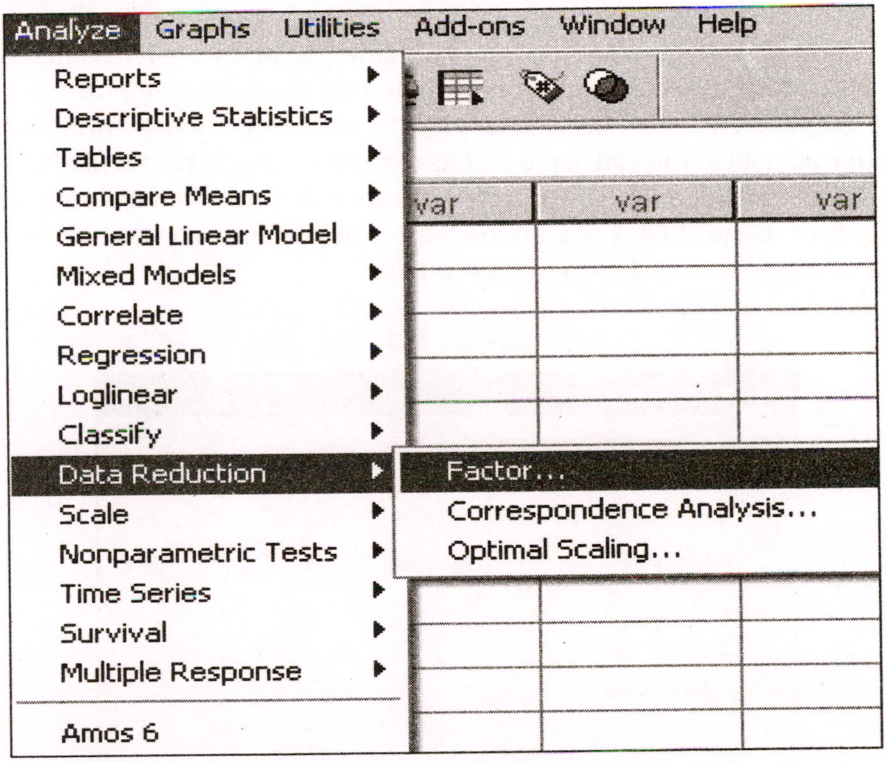

Figure 10.2

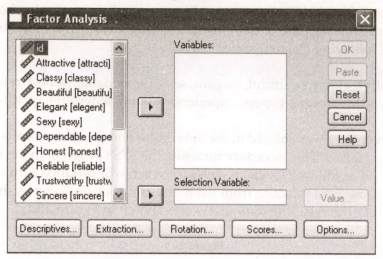

Select the variables from the left-hand side box and transfer them to the box labeled *Variables*. At the bottom of the box, there are five buttons. The first one labeled *Descriptives* gives you the option to choose various descriptive statistics. You can leave it at its default setting, which will give you the initial solution of FA. The other four buttons are important to understand the proper usage of FA. Click on the button labeled *Extraction* which brings up a dialogue box as shown in Figure 10.3.

Figure 10.3

There are many extraction methods listed, which can be obtained by clicking on the drop down arrow in the box against *Method*. Two commonly used extraction methods are *Principal Components* and *Principal Axis Factoring*. As discussed earlier, *Principal Components* is a data reduction technique and not strictly an FA technique. However, since the same is given in most of the programs as one of the extraction technique, people often confuse it with FA. Typically, if there is no mention of an extraction method in FA, one should assume that *Principal Axis Factoring* has been used. We have selected *Principal Axis Factoring* in this case. Next, we have to select whether we want to analyze the correlation matrix or the covariance matrix for FA. The recommended option for beginners is to use the correlation matrix, advanced users may, however, choose the covariance matrix for special cases. Click against *Unrotated factor solution* and *Scree plot* to display the two in the output. At the bottom of this box, we can specify the number of factors we want to extract. Default setting is to choose factors with eigenvalues greater than 1 as factors with eigenvalues less than 1 do not carry enough information. We can also specify the number of factors if we have a specific requirement to extract a certain number of factors. This is not advisable though, as the analysis in this case becomes purely mathematical. Click on *Continue* to return to the main dialogue box. Next, click on the button labeled *Rotation*, to specify the specific rotation strategy you want to adopt. This brings up a dialogue box as shown in Figure 10.4.

Figure 10.4

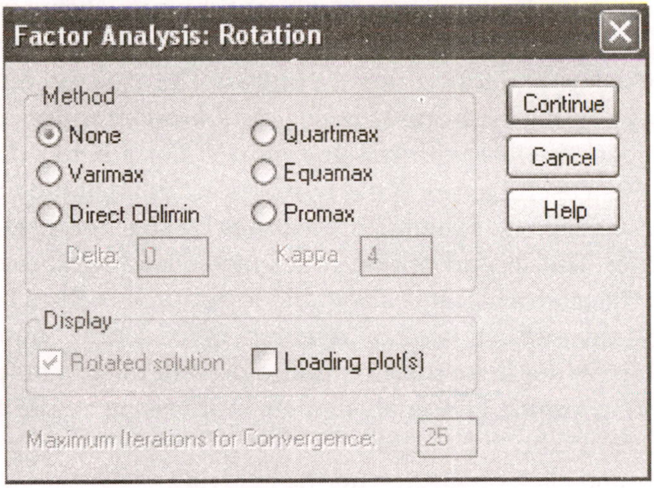

The SPSS program gives five options for rotations. Select *Varimax* from this box and click against *Rotated solution*. Readers are encouraged to try other rotation methods. In most of the cases, there is not much difference in the factor solutions obtained from different rotation methods. Click on *Continue* to return to the main dialogue box.

Next, click on the button labeled *Scores*. From the resulting dialogue box as shown in Figure 10.5, we can choose to save scores for each factor in our data set. These scores get saved for each observation as a new variable, which can be used for regression analysis as a composite measure of underlying dimensions. We did not choose to do so in our example as it is not related to our understanding of the FA technique and its output.

Figure 10.5

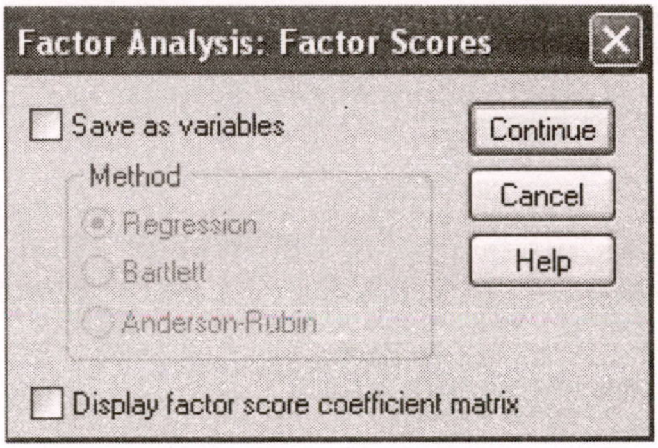

Finally click on the button labeled *Options*, which will bring up a dialogue box as shown in Figure 10.6. Here we can choose options for treating cases with missing values and formatting the output. The choice of missing values should always be the first one (*Exclude cases listwise*) unless one has any specific approach to deal with missing values. For a better display of the output, it is often useful to select the two options listed at the bottom of this box. The first option sorts the factor loadings by size and lists variables in the same order. The second option hides factor loadings below the value specified by the researcher. It is advisable to suppress values below 0.40 as this is a standard criterion used by researchers to identify important factor loadings. We have not done this in order to present the full output. Readers are advised to try running the analysis after suppressing values and compare the ease of reading the two outputs. Click on *Continue* to return to the main dialogue box and click on *OK* to run the analysis.

Figure 10.6

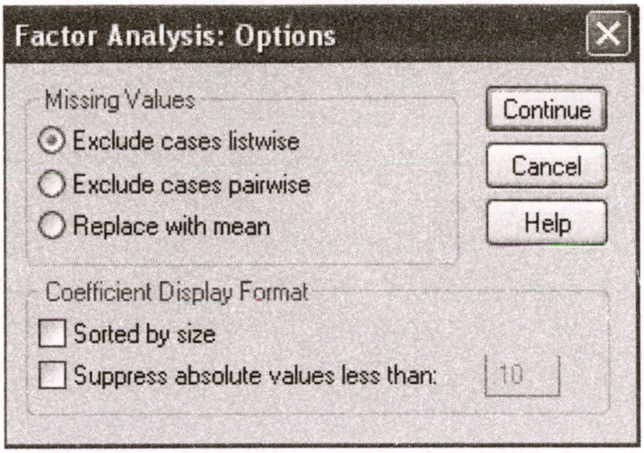

Output

SPSS displays FA output in many tables depending on what we specify while selecting various options. These results are shown in Figures 10.7 to 10.12. The first table titled *Communalities* (Figure 10.7) gives the initial and extraction communalities.

Figure 10.7

Factor Analysis

Communalities

	Initial	Extraction
Attractive	.523	.430
Classy	.498	.385
Beautiful	.676	.908
Elegant	.438	.303
Sexy	.467	.229
Dependable	.864	.803
Honest	.912	.907
Reliable	.888	.823
Trustworthy	.913	.839
Sincere	.852	.777
Skilled	.607	.469
Expert	.693	.613
Experienced	.641	.593
Knowledgeable	.814	.819
Qualified	.803	.831

Extraction Method: Principal Axis Factoring.

The extraction communalities are useful as these are obtained using the extracted factors. Extraction communalities for a variable give the total amount of variance in that variable, explained by all the factors. In our example, 90.84% of the variance in *beautiful* is explained by the extracted factors. If a particular variable has low communality, it means that the extracted factors are not able to explain much variance in that variable. Such variables may be dropped from the analysis.

The next table titled *Total Variance Explained* (Figure 10.8) summarizes the total variance explained by the FA solution and gives an indication about the number of useful factors. This table has three parts. The first part, titled *Initial Eigenvalues* gives the variance explained by all the possible factors. There are a total of 14 factors, which is same as the number of variables entered into the FA. However, please note that these factors are not the same as the variables. The first column under *Initial Eigenvalues* gives the eigenvalues for all the possible factors in a decreasing order. This is followed by the variance as a percentage of all the variance and cumulative variance. By simple computation, one can verify that the total variance explained is equal to the total number of factors (or variables), 14 in this case; and the percentage of variance for the first factor will be same as its eigenvalue divided by total variance.

The second part, titled *Extraction Sums of Squared Loadings* gives information for factors with eigenvalues greater than 1. The word "extraction" here refers to the fact that these values are calculated after factor extraction. In case of principal component analysis, these will be the same as initial eigenvalues. The figure under the column *Cumulative%* in this part indicates that the three extracted factors explain 64.87% of the variance.

The last part titled, *Rotated Sums of Squared Loadings* gives the information for extracted factors after rotation. Please note that after rotation, only the relative value of eigenvalues has changed, the cumulative percentage remains the same.

There are only three factors with eigenvalues greater than 1 suggesting a three-factor solution. Sometimes we may find eigenvalues of some of the factors dropping below 1 after rotation. A judgement has to be made in such cases about the number of factors to be extracted.

The scree plot shown in Figure 10.9 is another way of identifying the number of useful factors. We look for a sharp break in sizes of eigenvalues

Figure 10.8

Total Variance Explained

Factor	Initial Eigenvalues			Extraction Sums of Squared Loadings			Rotation Sums of Squared Loadings		
	Total	% of Variance	Cumulative %	Total	% of Variance	Cumulative %	Total	% of Variance	Cumulative %
1	6.201	41.337	41.337	5.952	39.683	39.683	4.490	29.934	29.934
2	2.398	15.984	57.321	1.977	13.183	52.866	3.197	21.314	51.247
3	2.064	13.760	71.081	1.800	12.001	64.867	2.043	13.620	64.867
4	.985	6.564	77.646						
5	.796	5.305	82.950						
6	.604	4.024	86.975						
7	.445	2.969	89.944						
8	.402	2.677	92.621						
9	.277	1.846	94.467						
10	.245	1.633	96.100						
11	.225	1.502	97.602						
12	.153	1.023	98.625						
13	.094	.628	99.253						
14	.065	.436	99.688						
15	.047	.312	100.000						

Extraction Method: Principal Axis Factoring.

which results in a change in the slope of the plot from steep to shallow. We can see that the slope of the scree plot changes from steep to shallow after the first three factors. The eigenvalue also drops from above two to less than one when we move from factor 3 to factor 4. This suggests that a three-factor solution may be the right choice.

Figure 10.9

Scree Plot

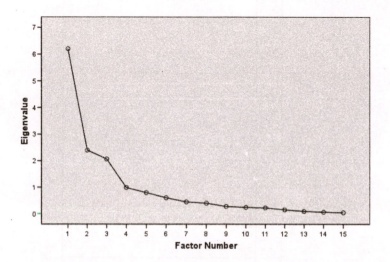

The next table titled *Factor Matrix* (Figure 10.10) gives the factor loadings before rotation is carried out. For each of the variables, we get a loading in each of the columns representing factors. The variables are listed in the decreasing order of factor loadings as we requested the same in the *Options* window. The extraction communalities presented in the second column of Figure 10.7 is a summation of the square of loadings on all the factors for a particular variable. For example, the extraction communality value for *Honest* in Figure 10.7 can be obtained as:

$$(0.878)^2 + (-0.071)^2 + (-0.368)^2 = 0.91$$

The factor loadings in the factor matrix are not easily interpretable. We can see that the variable *Experienced* has high loadings of 0.527 and 0.558 on two factors. Likewise, there are many other variables with high loadings

Figure 10.10

Factor Matrix[a]

	Factor		
	1	2	3
Honest	.876	-.071	-.368
Reliable	.852	-.118	-.289
Trustworthy	.845	-.130	-.328
Dependable	.834	-.127	-.303
Sincere	.806	-.168	-.314
Qualified	.708	.058	.572
Knowledgeable	.675	-.036	.601
Skilled	.671	-.006	.138
Expert	.654	.003	.431
Classy	.434	.429	-.110
Beautiful	.151	.937	-.083
Attractive	.066	.651	-.048
Sexy	-.037	.476	.030
Elegant	.269	.420	-.235
Experienced	.527	.063	.558

Extraction Method: Principal Axis Factoring.

a. 3 factors extracted. 15 iterations required.

on more than one factor in the factor matrix. Rotation sometimes solves this problem. Figure 10.11 presents the table titled *Rotated Factor Matrix* which has rotated loadings. For a good factor solution, a particular variable should load high on one factor and low on all other factors in the rotated factor matrix. Researchers commonly use a cut-off of 0.40 to identify high loadings. In this example, we can see that the variables which are loading high on factor 1 have low loadings on factors 2 and 3. Likewise, those loading high on other factors have low loadings on the remaining factors. This is close to being an ideal situation. In case we find a variable loading high on more than one factor, we may want to drop it from the analyses and make revisions based on theoretical considerations.

Once we obtain the variables corresponding to particular factors, we may give suitable names to the factors. For example, in this case factor 1 comprises five variables—*Honest*, *Trustworthy*, *Reliable*, *Sincere* and *Dependable*; factor 2

Figure 10.11

Rotated Factor Matrix[a]

	Factor		
	1	2	3
Honest	.925	.207	.091
Trustworthy	.889	.220	.024
Reliable	.870	.256	.032
Dependable	.865	.233	.022
Sincere	.857	.207	-.020
Knowledgeable	.208	.880	-.022
Qualified	.234	.878	.078
Experienced	.096	.762	.061
Expert	.280	.730	.035
Skilled	.462	.501	.065
Beautiful	.001	.044	.952
Attractive	-.036	.016	.655
Classy	.335	.174	.493
Elegant	.274	-.025	.477
Sexy	-.132	.015	.460

Extraction Method: Principal Axis Factoring.
Rotation Method: Varimax with Kaiser Normalization.

a. Rotation converged in 5 iterations.

comprises four variables—*Knowledgeable, Qualified, Experienced* and *Expert*; factor 3 comprises five variables—*Beautiful, Attractive, Classy, Elegant* and *Sexy*. These three factors can be clubbed together and termed "*Trustworthiness, Expertise* and *Attractiveness.*"

The last table titled *Factor Transformation Matrix* is only for the purpose of providing information. This matrix is used for carrying out the rotation. It is of no use for the interpretation of results.

Figure 10.12

Factor Transformation Matrix

Factor	1	2	3
1	.804	.580	.131
2	-.179	.026	.984
3	-.567	.814	-.124

Extraction Method: Principal Axis Factoring.
Rotation Method: Varimax with Kaiser Normalization.

If we perform the principal component analysis in the place of principal axis factoring, we will see the word "Component" in the place of "Factor" in the output.

SYNTAX

The syntax for obtaining the above output is given below:

```
FACTOR
/VARIABLES attracti classy beautifu elegent sexy dependab honest reliable
trustwor sincere expert experien knowledg qualifie
/MISSING LISTWISE /ANALYSIS attracti classy beautifu elegent sexy
dependab honest reliable trustwor sincere expert experien knowledg qualifie
/PRINT INITIAL EXTRACTION ROTATION
/FORMAT SORT BLANK(.40)
/PLOT EIGEN
/CRITERIA MINEIGEN(1) ITERATE(25)
/EXTRACTION PAF
/CRITERIA ITERATE(25)
/ROTATION VARIMAX
/METHOD=CORRELATION .
```

10.2.2 Scale Reliability

In the factor analysis example, we found three factors which we termed as *Trustworthiness*, *Expertise* and *Attractiveness*. It will be premature to claim that the underlying items of these factors make up the scale for measuring these factors. But for the purpose of illustration, we will assume this to be correct. Now we want to measure the reliability of these scales.

Open the data file for Example 10.1. Click on *Analyze*, which will produce a drop down menu, choose *Scale* from that and click on *Reliability Analysis* as shown in Figure 10.13. The resulting dialogue box is shown in Figure 10.14.

Figure 10.13

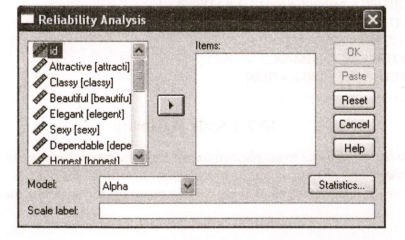

Figure 10.14

We can test the reliability of only one scale at a time. We illustrate here the reliability testing for the scale on *Trustworthiness*. Select the items used to measure *Trustworthiness* and transfer them to the box labeled *Items*. The *Trustworthiness* scale items include *dependable, honest, reliable, trustworthy,* and *sincere*. Click on the button labeled *Statistics* which will open a dialogue box as shown in Figure 10.15.

Select the descriptive statistics for *Item, Scale* and *Scale if item deleted*. Click on *Continue* to return to the main dialogue box and click on *OK* to run the analysis.

Figure 10.15

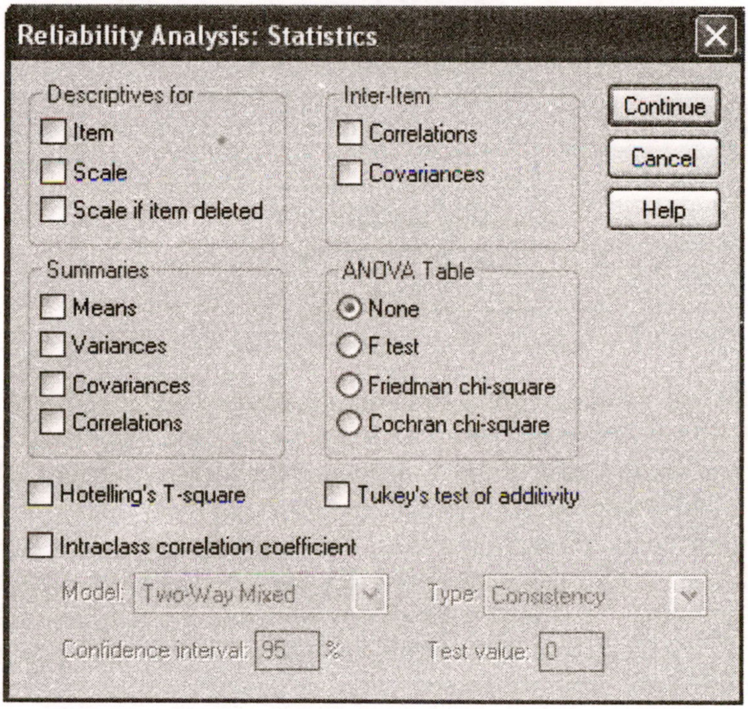

Output

The output is shown in Figures 10.16 and 10.17. In Figure 10.16, the first table titled *Case Processing Summary* gives the description of cases selected for analysis. The second table titled *Reliability Statistics* gives the value of the Cronbach alpha coefficient and the number of items selected for the scale. For our scale of *Trustworthiness*, we find the Cronbach alpha value to be 0.96.

Figure 10.16

Reliability

Scale: ALL VARIABLES

Case Processing Summary

		N	%
Cases	Valid	56	100.0
	Excluded[a]	0	.0
	Total	56	100.0

a. Listwise deletion based on all variables in the procedure.

Reliability Statistics

Cronbach's Alpha	N of Items
.960	5

We also get the descriptive statistics as shown in Figure 10.17. The first table titled *Item Statistics* gives item-wise mean and standard deviation values. The second table titled *Item-Total Statistics* is important. The fourth column in this table, titled *Corrected Item-Total Correlation* gives an indication of the degree to which each item correlates with the composite score for the scale. The last column labeled *Cronbach's Alpha if Item Deleted* gives the impact of removing each item on the alpha coefficient. Looking at these values, along with the Cronbach alpha coefficient values, one may decide to remove some of the items from the scale.

Figure 10.17

Item Statistics

	Mean	Std. Deviation	N
Dependable	3.41	1.023	56
Honest	3.34	.996	56
Reliable	3.21	1.074	56
Trustworthy	3.21	1.107	56
Sincere	3.36	1.034	56

Item-Total Statistics

	Scale Mean if Item Deleted	Scale Variance if Item Deleted	Corrected Item-Total Correlation	Cronbach's Alpha if Item Deleted
Dependable	13.13	15.711	.853	.956
Honest	13.20	15.470	.920	.946
Reliable	13.32	15.022	.900	.949
Trustworthy	13.32	14.695	.913	.947
Sincere	13.18	15.604	.856	.956

Scale Statistics

Mean	Variance	Std. Deviation	N of Items
16.54	23.671	4.865	5

SYNTAX

The syntax for obtaining the above output is given below:

```
RELIABILITY
/VARIABLES=dependab honest reliable trustwor sincere
/FORMAT=NOLABELS
/SCALE(ALPHA)=ALL/MODEL=ALPHA
/STATISTICS=DESCRIPTIVE SCALE
/SUMMARY=TOTAL .
```

Table 10.1

Data for Example 10.1

Id	qualified	knowledgeable	experienced	expert	sincere	trustworthy	reliable	honest	dependable	sexy	elegant	beautiful	classy	attractive
1	2	2	3	4	4	3	4	4	5	5	5	5	4	4
2	3	5	3	3	3	3	3	4	3	5	5	5	5	5
3	3	3	3	3	3	3	3	3	3	5	4	5	3	5
4	3	4	2	4	4	4	4	4	4	4	5	4	5	4
5	5	4	4	4	2	2	2	2	3	4	5	5	5	5
6	2	4	2	2	2	2	2	2	2	5	5	5	5	5
7	4	4	1	4	1	1	1	2	1	5	4	4	2	5
8	3	3	3	4	4	4	4	4	4	5	5	5	5	5
9	2	2	2	2	3	3	3	3	3	5	4	5	4	5
10	4	5	3	4	2	2	4	5	5	5	5	5	5	5
11	3	3	3	3	3	3	3	3	3	5	4	5	3	5
12	3	3	4	4	3	3	3	3	3	5	3	5	5	5
13	3	3	4	4	3	2	2	2	2	4	4	5	4	5
14	3	3	3	3	4	4	4	4	4	5	5	4	5	5
15	3	2	1	4	3	1	1	2	3	3	4	4	4	5
16	4	4	4	4	4	4	4	4	4	4	5	4	4	4
17	5	3	3	4	5	4	3	4	5	3	4	3	3	4
18	4	4	4	3	5	5	5	5	5	1	2	4	4	4
19	4	3	3	4	4	4	4	4	4	3	4	4	4	4
20	3	3	4	3	4	4	4	4	4	5	5	4	4	4
21	3	3	3	5	2	2	2	2	2	4	3	4	4	4
22	5	5	3	5	5	5	5	5	5	3	5	5	5	5
23	4	4	3	4	3	3	3	3	4	4	5	5	5	5
24	4	3	3	4	3	3	3	3	3	4	4	5	4	5
25	4	5	4	4	3	3	3	3	3	5	5	5	5	5

26	27	28	29	30	31	32	33	34	35	36	37	38	39	40	41	42	43	44	45	46	47	48	49	50	51	52	53	54	55	56
3	5	4	2	2	1	3	4	4	5	4	2	3	5	1	4	5	4	4	3	5	5	3	4	1	4	3	3	4	5	2
4	5	4	2	2	1	3	5	4	5	4	2	4	4	4	4	4	4	4	4	5	5	3	3	1	4	3	4	4	5	2
3	3	4	2	2	1	4	4	4	5	4	1	4	4	1	4	4	3	4	3	5	5	3	4	1	4	3	3	3	4	2
4	5	4	5	4	1	4	4	4	5	4	3	4	3	3	4	5	2	3	4	2	5	3	4	1	4	3	4	3	3	2
4	5	3	2	3	3	4	3	4	5	4	2	4	4	1	4	5	2	4	4	2	5	3	4	4	4	2	4	3	3	2
4	5	3	2	2	3	4	4	4	5	4	3	3	3	1	4	5	1	4	3	2	5	3	5	4	4	2	3	3	3	2
4	5	3	2	3	3	3	5	4	5	4	3	3	2	1	4	5	2	4	3	2	5	3	4	3	4	2	3	2	3	2
4	5	3	3	3	3	3	3	4	5	4	3	3	3	2	4	5	1	4	3	2	5	3	5	3	4	2	3	3	3	2
4	5	3	3	3	2	3	3	4	5	4	3	3	4	3	4	5	2	4	3	2	5	3	5	3	4	2	3	2	3	2
4	3	4	5	3	4	4	5	5	5	4	5	5	5	4	4	5	5	5	3	4	5	5	5	5	5	4	3	5	5	3
4	5	4	5	4	4	4	3	5	5	4	5	3	5	4	5	5	3	4	5	4	4	5	5	3	5	4	4	5	4	5
4	5	5	5	5	5	4	5	5	5	4	5	5	5	4	4	5	4	5	5	5	5	5	5	5	4	5	5	5	5	4
5	5	4	5	5	4	4	3	5	5	4	4	3	5	3	4	5	3	4	5	5	5	4	4	5	5	4	5	5	4	2
5	5	5	5	5	5	5	4	5	5	4	5	5	5	4	4	5	4	5	5	5	5	5	5	5	4	4	5	4	5	4

11

Advanced Data Handling in SPSS

In case of research based on secondary data, the number of cases may be quite large. Even in the case of survey and experimental research, it is not uncommon to have a few hundred cases. Researchers may need to run analyses on a subset of the cases or create new variables from the existing variables based on certain conditions. The commands described in this chapter are very useful for managing large and complex data files.

We use the data file of Example 3.1 given in Chapter 3 for illustration. We discuss the following data handling techniques in this chapter:

1) Sorting cases
2) Merging files
3) Aggregating cases
4) Splitting files
5) Selecting cases
6) Recoding
7) Computing new variables

All the commands used in this chapter are given under *Data* or *Transform* menus.

11.1 SORTING CASES

Normally, the order of responses does not matter while running an analysis. Still, sometimes we may be interested in having the data in a particular order in the editor window. This can be achieved by sorting files. In Example 3.1, if we want to see the responses in increasing order of respondents' *age* and decreasing order of *sales*, we can do this in the following manner.

Click on *Data* in the data editor window and select *Sort Cases* from the drop down menu as shown in Figure 11.1. This produces a dialogue box as shown in Figure 11.2. The ascending or descending order has to be chosen before transferring a variable into the *Sort by* box. Since we want the data to be in ascending order of age and descending order of sales, click on *Ascending* and transfer *age* into the box labeled *Sort by*. Next, click on *Descending* and transfer *sales* to the *Sort by* box. You may choose any number of variables to sort the data file. Click on *OK* and the data file will be sorted in the ascending order of *age* and descending order of *sales*.

Figure 11.1

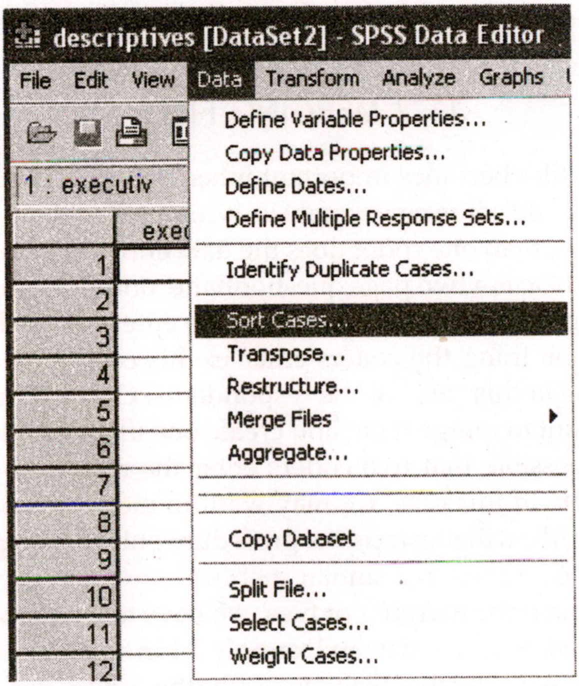

SYNTAX

The syntax for performing the above discussed sort command is given below:

SORT CASES BY
age (A) sales (D) .

Figure 11.2

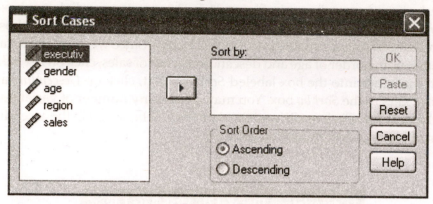

11.2 MERGING FILES

The merging of files becomes important when we have to add some cases to our data file or add some new variables. While coding data, it is a common practice that more than one coder does the data entry on a standard format. For example, if there is a two page questionnaire, one coder may be entering data for one page and the other coder may be entering for the other page. The only common thing the coders enter in this case is the identification number (*executiv* in this case) of the respondents. Once we have these two files, we may want to merge them and create one file with all the variables. Likewise, it is possible that two coders enter the responses of half of the respondents each. In this case, we may want to merge cases from the two files into one file. We will illustrate the procedure only for merging variables. Cases can also be merged in a similar manner.

Before we explain the merging of files, we have to create two files which have to be merged. Save the data in Example 3.1 in an SPSS file with the file name "descriptives1". In this file, keep only the *gender, age* and *region* information for each respondent. Create another file with the file name "descriptives2" and keep the sales data for each respondent in this file. Please note that both these files will have the *executiv* variable, which is nothing but a unique identifier for each respondent. It is this identifier variable, based on which the SPSS program will merge variables from the two files.

Before merging the two files, data in both the files should be sorted in ascending order by the "By" variable, which is the key variable used for merging the files. In this example, *executiv* is the "By" variable. Sort both the files by *executiv* as explained in the previous section and save the files. Now open the file into which you want to merge the variables—*descriptives1* in this case.

Click on *Data*, choose *Merge Files* from the drop down menu and click on *Add Variables* as shown in Figure 11.3. This produces a dialogue box (Figure 11.4). This dialogue box prompts you to select a data set from which you want to merge the variables of interest. The data set could be an already open data set or some external SPSS file. The dialogue box shown in Figure 11.4 does not come in earlier versions of SPSS, as one could not open multiple data editor windows. Clicking on *Browse* in the second option will take you to the folder in which you have stored the file into which you are merging the variables (*descriptives1*). You have to select the second file (*descriptives2*) from which you want to merge variables. In case the second file is not stored in the same folder as the first one, browse through folders as is done while opening any file and select the file. Once you select the second file, click *Continue* and a new dialogue box will open as shown in Figure 11.5.

Figure 11.3

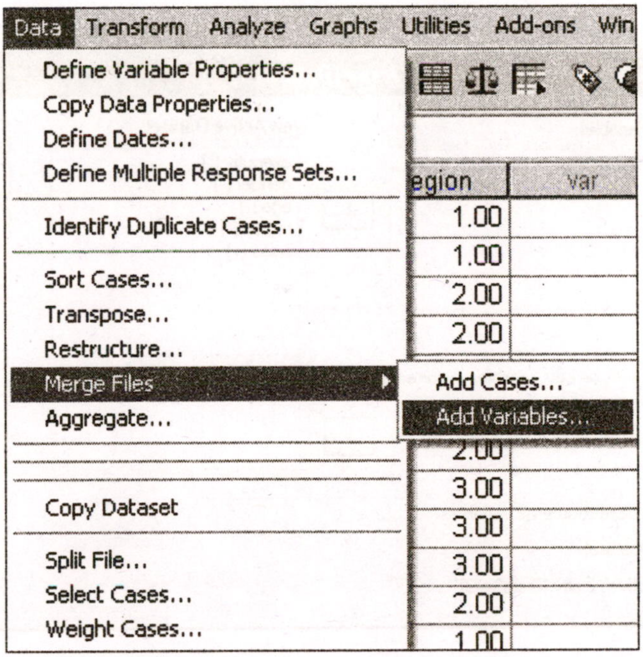

Figure 11.4

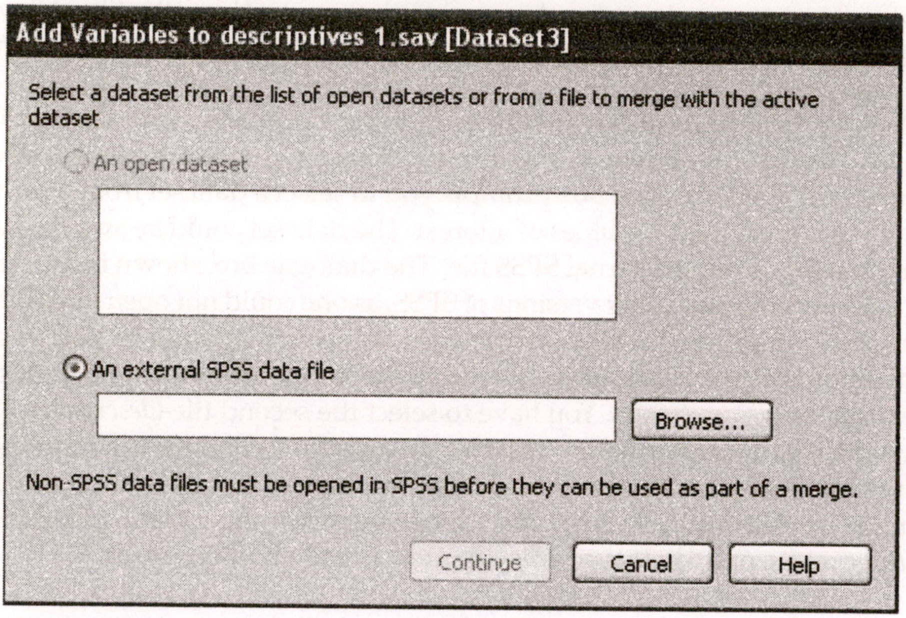

Figure 11.5

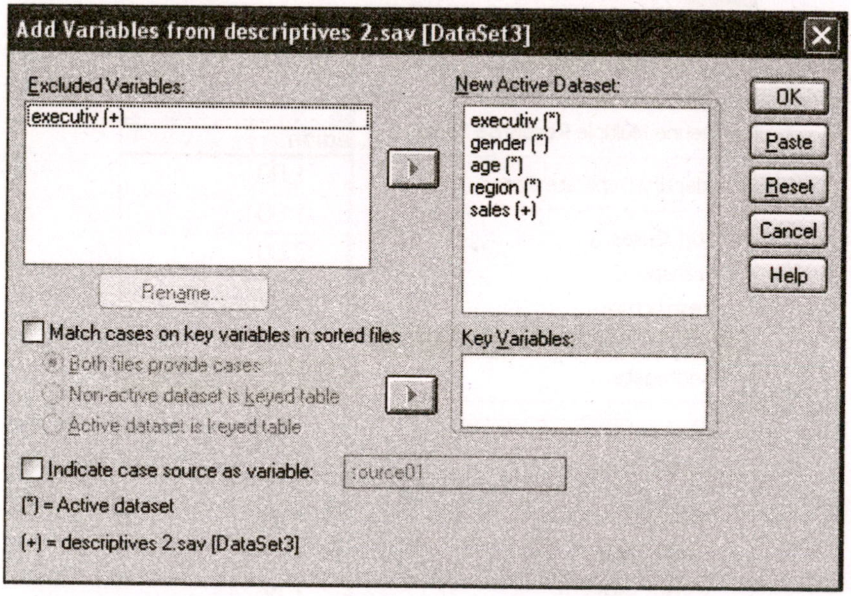

The right-hand side box labeled *Excluded Variables* lists the common variables in the two files. The left-hand side box labeled *New Active Dataset* lists the variables from both the files. To differentiate the variables from the two files, it puts * against the variables from the file into which we are merging the data and + against the variables which come from the external file. In this case, *sales* is the variable from the external file. If we do not want certain variables in the new file, we may discard them by selecting the variables from the right-hand side box and transferring them into the *Excluded Variables* box on the left-hand side.

Next, we have to specify the key variable by which we are matching the two files. In this case it is *executiv*. Select the key variable (*executiv*) and tick in the box against *Match cases on key variables in sorted files*. This activates the three sub-options below it. Select the *External file is keyed table* and transfer the *executiv* into the box labeled *Key Variables*. This will essentially ask SPSS to match sales values from the second file by the respondent's ids. We may specify more than one key variable. Click on *OK*, and you will see a warning that the matching will fail if the data is not sorted in an ascending order. Click on *OK* again to complete the merging. You can check the data file to see that the variable *sales* is added in the *descriptives1* file.

SYNTAX

The syntax for performing the merging in the given example follows:

```
MATCH FILES /FILE=*
/TABLE='E:\AAA\india\SPSS\data files\descriptives 2.sav'
/BY executiv.
EXECUTE.
```

The second row here specifies the file from which data is to be merged.

11.3 AGGREGATING CASES

The aggregate command may not be very useful for small data files, but becomes essential while working with large files. By running an Aggregate command, we create a new data file with the variables specified by us. The illustration given in this section will make this point clear.

Supposing in Example 3.1, we are only interested in region-wise sales values. Click on *Data* in the data editor window and select *Aggregate* from the drop down menu as shown in Figure 11.1. This produces a dialogue box as shown in Figure 11.6.

Figure 11.6

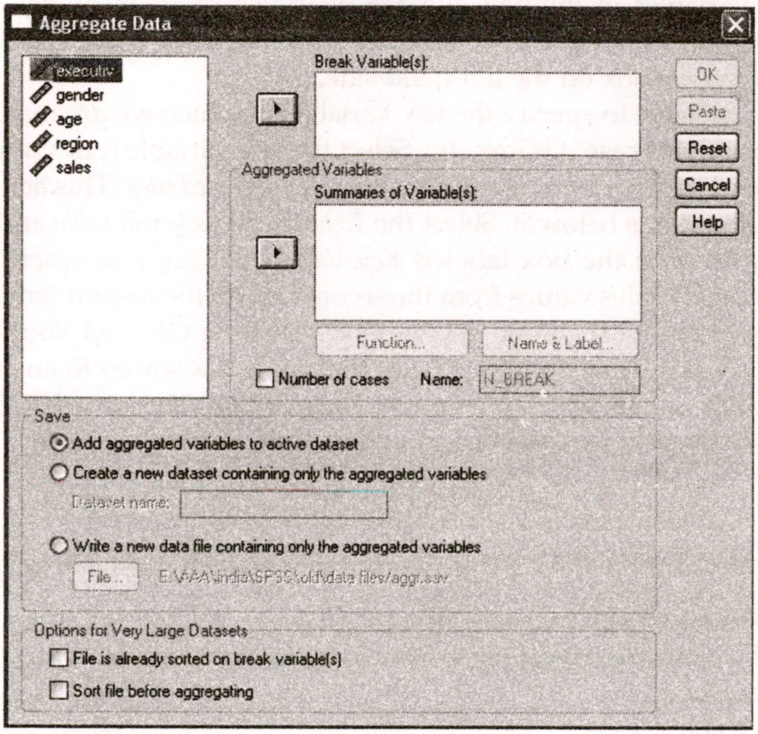

We have to specify the variables by which we want to aggregate our data in the *Break Variable(s)* box. In our example, since we want the data to be aggregated by regions, select and transfer *region* into the *Break Variable(s)* box. Next, we have to specify the variables which we want to aggregate into the box labeled *Summaries of Variable(s)*. Select *sales* and transfer it into this box. Once the summary variables are transferred, two additional buttons become active below this box. Click on the button labeled *Function* which opens a dialogue box (Figure 11.7). We can specify the way we want to aggregate the data from this box. The default setting is for mean, which will give you the mean of the sales value for all the regions. One can also choose to produce some specific values such as minimum, maximum etc. We let the default setting stay as it is and click on *Continue* to return to the main dialogue box (Figure 11.6).

Figure 11.7

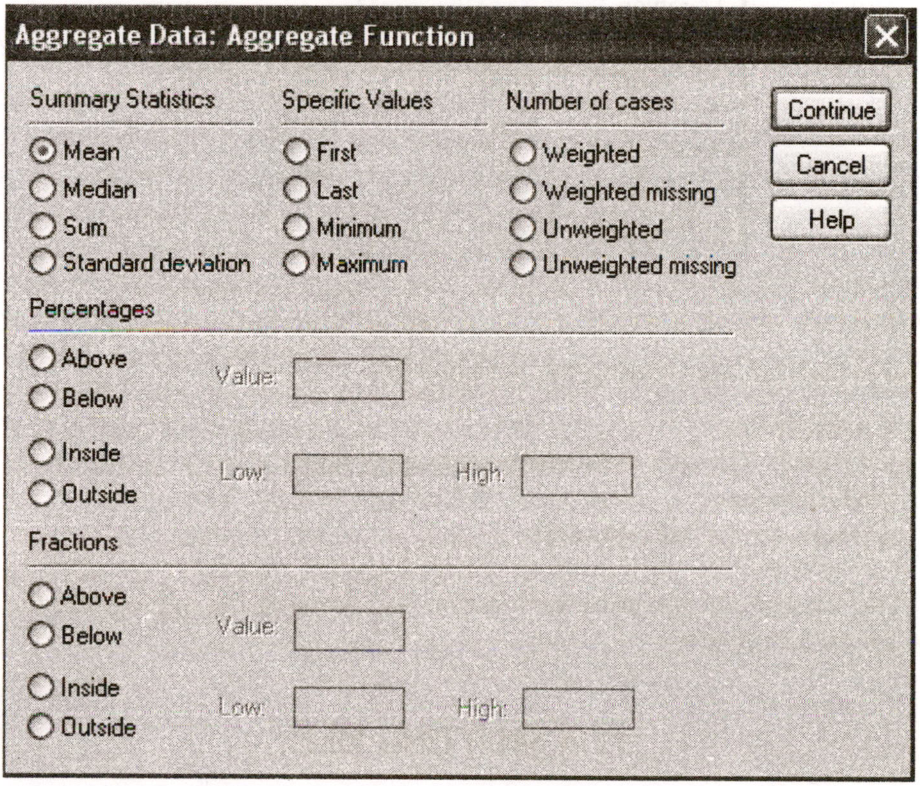

Next, we can specify whether we want to add the aggregated variables to the current data file, create a new data set with only the aggregated variables or store the aggregated variables in a new file. We select to store the data into a new file. This will save the aggregated data into a file named "aggr.sav" in the same location as the current working file. These settings can be changed. If you open the aggregated file, you will see three rows corresponding to three regions and two variables as shown in Figure 11.8.

Figure 11.8

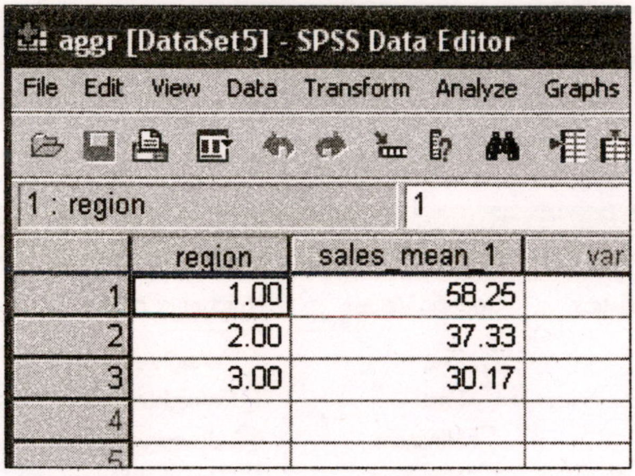

SYNTAX

The syntax for aggregating the variables is:

AGGREGATE
/OUTFILE='E:\AAA\india\SPSS\data files/aggr.sav'
/BREAK=region
/sales_mean_1 = MEAN(sales).

The second row specifies the location and name of the aggregated file to be saved as a new file.

11.4 SPLITTING FILES

The Split File command temporarily splits the file into groups. All the analyses done after splitting a file will be done separately on the different subgroups and the output will be arranged according to these groups. For example, if we are interested in obtaining descriptive statistics about age and sales by gender, we can split the file by the *gender* variable.

Click on *Data* in the data editor window and select *Split File* from the drop down menu as shown in Figure 11.1. This produces a dialogue box as shown in Figure 11.9.

Figure 11.9

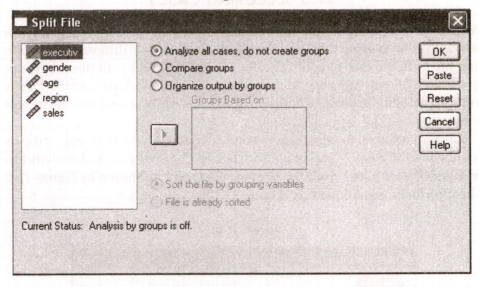

The default option in this window is to analyze all the cases. Select *Compare groups* or *Organize output by groups*. The first option presents the output within one section, comparing the groups, while the second option presents the output in different sections. Selecting either of these will activate the box labeled *Groups Based on*. Select *gender* and transfer to this box. Click on *OK* to complete splitting the file. Now if you run any analysis, two outputs will be produced, one for males and the other for females.

Splitting file is a temporary option and you can cancel it by selecting *Analyze all cases, do not create groups*.

SYNTAX

The syntax for splitting file by *gender* is given below:

SORT CASES BY gender .
SPLIT FILE
SEPARATE BY gender .

11.5 SELECTING CASES

We can run our analyses in a sub-sample of the total cases by specifying our selection criteria using the *Select Cases* command. This is different from splitting file as in the case of splitting a file, we get output by all the subgroups specified by a particular variable. In the split command, we cannot specify multiple selection criteria. In addition, splitting a file by a continuous variable is meaningless.

Suppose we want to select a sub-sample of cases in which the age of the respondents is at least 22 years or above. Click on *Data* in the data editor window and select *Select Cases* from the drop down menu as shown in Figure 11.1. This produces a dialogue box (Figure 11.10).

Figure 11.10

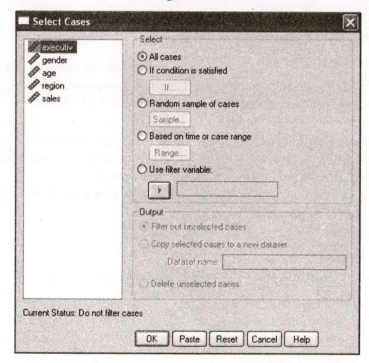

The default setting is to run the analyses for all the cases. Tick against *If condition is satisfied*, this will activate the button labeled *If* below it. Click on

If, which opens a dialogue box as shown in Figure 11.11. In this dialogue box, we have to specify the selection criteria. Since we want respondents with at least 22 years of age, our selection criterion will be: *age>* = 22. Select *age* and transfer it to the right-hand side box and specify this selection criterion using the options given at the bottom of this box. We can also type multiple selection criteria in this box. For example, if we want to select a respondent over 27 years or below 25 years and belonging to region 1, we can specify the following formula:

$$(age>27 \ or \ age<25) \ and \ region = 1$$

Figure 11.11

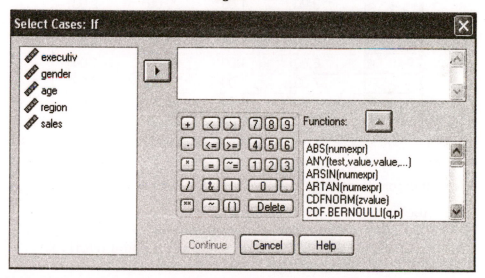

Click on *Continue* to return to the main dialogue box (Figure 11.10). We can also specify whether we want to filter out the unselected cases from analyses, copy selected cases to a new data set, or delete the unselected cases from the file. It is advisable not to delete the cases as you may need the unselected cases for future analyses. We choose the first option to filter out the unselected cases. Click on *OK* to complete the selection. The data editor window looks as shown in Figure 11.12. SPSS puts a cross line through the case number which is not selected. One can revert back to analyzing all the cases by selecting *All cases* from the main dialogue box (Figure 11.10).

Figure 11.12

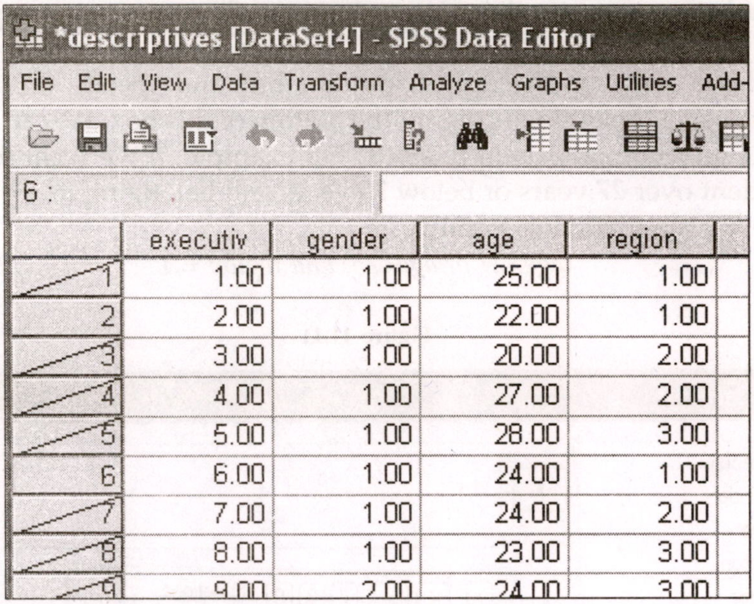

	executiv	gender	age	region
1	1.00	1.00	25.00	1.00
2	2.00	1.00	22.00	1.00
3	3.00	1.00	20.00	2.00
4	4.00	1.00	27.00	2.00
5	5.00	1.00	28.00	3.00
6	6.00	1.00	24.00	1.00
7	7.00	1.00	24.00	2.00
8	8.00	1.00	23.00	3.00
9	9.00	2.00	24.00	3.00

SYNTAX

The syntax for specifying the above selection criteria is given below:

```
USE ALL.
COMPUTE filter_$=(age>27 or age<25 and region=1).
VARIABLE LABEL filter_$ 'age>27 or age<25 and region=1 (FILTER)'.
VALUE LABELS filter_$ 0 'Not Selected' 1 'Selected'.
FORMAT filter_$ (f1.0).
FILTER BY filter_$.
EXECUTE .
```

11.6 RECODING VALUES

Many times, we may want to recode some of the variables. This could be because we may obtain data in different format from surveys or secondary resources and we may have to put them in a certain format for the purpose of analyses. For example, we may want to create two categories of respondents in the first example—one with age less than or equal to 25 years

and the other with age greater than 25. We may also want to recode some values to missing values. The illustration below describes these options.

Click on *Transform* in the data editor window and select *Recode* from the drop down menu as shown in Figure 11.13. The SPSS program gives two options to recode. The *Into Same Variables* option replaces the current values with the recoded values. The *Into Different Variables* option creates a new variable. It is advisable to always recode into a new variable so that we can avoid the loss of original data in case of a wrong recode command. If a variable is recoded into the same variable and the new file saved, there is no way we can get back the original variable. Click on *Into Different Variables* which produces a dialogue box as shown in Figure 11.14.

Figure 11.13

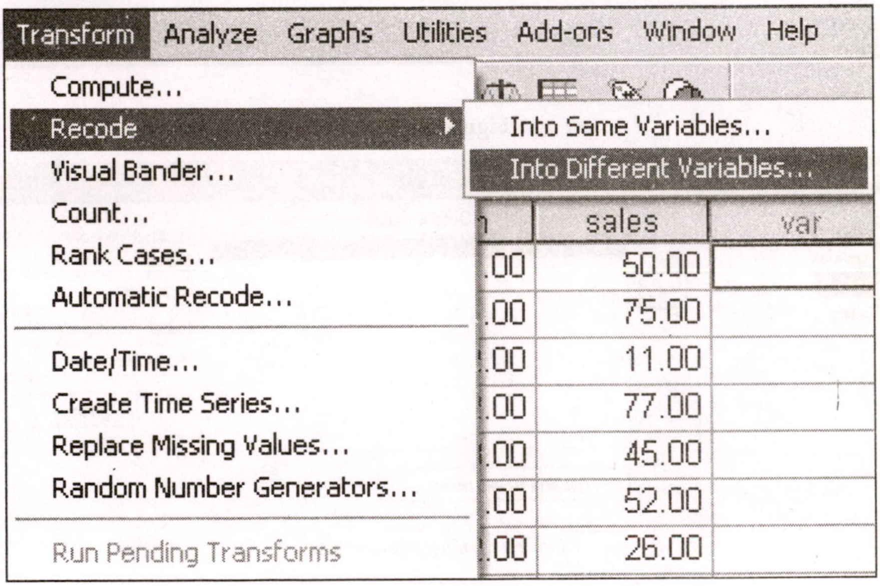

Select *age* and transfer it into the box labeled *Input Variable → Output Variable*. Once this is done, two boxes on the left-hand side become active. We have to specify the name and label of the new variable in these boxes. Type *age_cat* in the box labeled *Name* and *Age Category* as its label in the box labeled *Label*. Now click on the button labeled *Change* to transfer the name of the output variable into the box labeled *Input variable → Output variable*. The resulting dialogue box appears as shown in Figure 11.15.

Figure 11.14

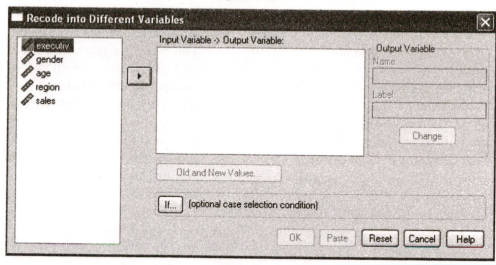

Figure 11.15

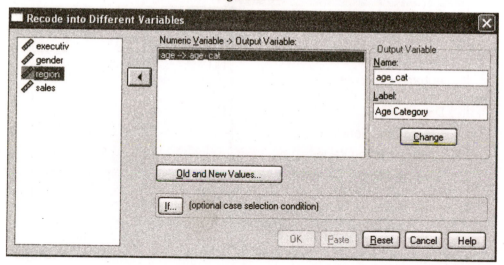

Next, click on the box labeled *Old and New Values* which produces a dialogue box as shown in Figure 11.16. In this box, we have to specify our recoding strategy which is to recode age less than or equal to 25 as a zero, and more than 25 as one.

To specify the first range, tick against *Range, LOWEST through value* and specify 25 in the box opposite to it. Next, specify zero in the left-hand side box against *Value*. Click on *Add* to transfer these values to the box labeled *Old -> New*. In a similar manner specify the second range in the box *Range, value through HIGHEST*, specify 1 as the value for this range in the *Value* box and click on *Add*. The resulting dialogue box appears as shown in Figure 11.17. Click on *Continue* to return to the main dialogue box (Figure 11.15).

We can further specify some selection criteria for running the recode command on a sub-sample of cases. This can be done by clicking on the button labeled *If* as explained in the previous section. Click on *OK* to complete the recoding exercise. A new variable named *age_cat* is created in the data file, which takes a value of 0 for age less than or equal to 25 years and 1 for age greater than 25 years.

SYNTAX

The syntax for the recoding is given below:

```
RECODE
age
(Lowest thru 25=0) (26 thru Highest=1) INTO age_cat .
VARIABLE LABELS age_cat 'Age Category'.
EXECUTE .
```

Figure 11.17

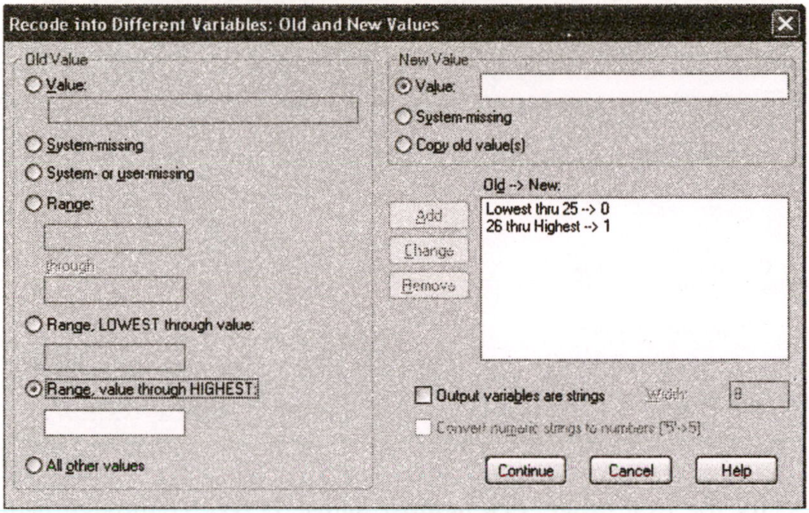

11.7 COMPUTING NEW VARIABLES

Quite often we need to create many new variables from the original variables on which we collect the data. A very common usage is to create an interaction term while performing moderated regression analysis. Suppose we want to create an interaction between age and gender.

Click on *Transform* in the data editor window and select *Compute* from the drop down menu as shown in Figure 11.13. This produces a dialogue box (Figure 11.18). Specify the name of the variable to be created in the *Target Variable* box and specify the numerical expression in the box labeled *Numeric Expression*. We can indicate the type and label of the variable by clicking on the button labeled *Type & Label*. We can either type the expressions or select the variables and use appropriate buttons to specify the expression. For creating an interaction term between age and gender, we create the following expression:

$$gen\_age = gender*age$$

The selection criteria can also be specified at the bottom of box. Click on *OK* to complete the computation of the new variable. In the data file, a new variable named *gen_age* is created.

Figure 11.18

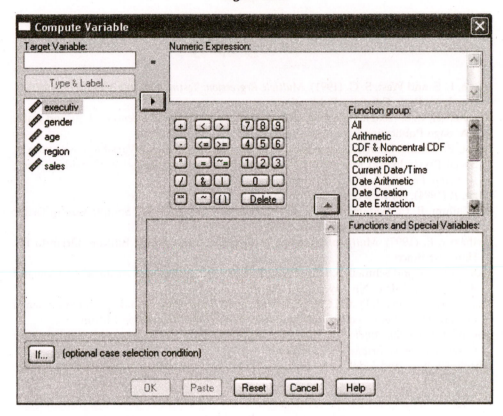

SYNTAX

The syntax for computing an interaction between gender and age is given below:

```
COMPUTE gen_age = gender * age .
EXECUTE .
```

Bibliography

Aiken, L. S. and West, S. G. (1991). *Multiple Regression: Testing and Interpreting Interactions*. Newbury Park, CA: Sage Publications.

Aneshensel, C. S. (2002). *Theory-Based Data Analysis for the Social Sciences*. Thousand Oaks, CA: Sage Publications.

Baron, R. M. and Kenny, D. A. (1986). "The Moderator-Mediator Variable Distinction in Social Psychological Research: Conceptual, Strategic, and Statistical Considerations", *Journal of Personality and Social Psychology*, 51: 1173–82.

Kline, P. (1994). *An Easy Guide to Factor Analysis*. London: Routledge.

MacCallum, R. C., Widaman, K. F., Zhang, S. and Hong, S. (1999). Sample Size in Factor Analysis. *Psychological Methods*. 4: 84–99.

Pedhazur, E. (1997). *Multiple Regression in Behavior Research*, 3rd Edition. Orlando FL: Harcourt Brace.

Pedhazur, E. J. and Schmelkin, L. P. (1991). *Measurement, Design, and Analysis: An Integrated Approach*. Hillsdale, NJ: Lawrence Erlbaum.

Shadish, W. R., Cook, T. D. and Campbell, D. T. (2002). Experimental and Quasi-Experimental Designs for Generalized Causal Inference. Boston, MA: Houghton Mifflin.

Stevens, J. P. (2002). *Applied Multivariate Statistics for the Social Sciences*, 4th Edition. New Jersey: Lawrence Erlbaum Associates.

Tebachnick B. G. and Fidell L. S. (2001). *Using Multivariate Statistics*, 2nd Edition. Boston: Allyn and Bacon.

About the Authors

Ajai S. Gaur is currently at the Department of Business Policy, National University of Singapore (NUS). He holds a Ph.D. in Management, a Masters degree in International Business and a B. Tech. in Mining engineering.

Dr Gaur taught at the Indian Institute of Foreign Trade from 2000 to 2003. He has been visiting faculty at leading business schools and has conducted workshops on research methods and strategy for doctoral students as well as faculty members at many institutions. His research interests lie at the intersection of strategy and international business. His work has been presented in leading conferences such as the Academy of Management, and Academy of International Business and Strategic Management Society. He has also published several research papers in national and international journals.

Sanjaya S. Gaur is currently at the Shailesh J. Mehta School of Management, Indian Institute of Technology, Bombay. He is also an Adjunct Professor at the University of Hoseo and SIT University in South Korea. He has been a Visiting Research Professor at LiU School of Management, Linköping University, Sweden; a Visiting Professor at the Graduate School of Venture, University of Hoseo, South Korea; and a Visiting Scholar at Marketing Centrum Muenster, Westphalian Wilhelms University (WWU), Muenster, Germany.

Dr Gaur is a frequent speaker on topics related to marketing and participates regularly at international and national conferences. He has previously written *Event Marketing and Management* (2001) and published several research papers in national and international journals. His experience extends beyond teaching and research to consulting and corporate training. He has been a consultant to several Indian and multinational companies such as Johnson & Johnson, HSBC, Ranbaxy Laboratories Limited, RFCL, Geologistics India Ltd, and Godrej and Boyce Manufacturing Co. Ltd.

COUPON FOR SPSS TRIAL SOFTWARE
FOR STATISTICAL ANALYSIS

SPSS

Get Free!
SPSS Trial Software

Name _____

Title/Department _____

Organisation _____

Address _____

City _____ Pin _____

Phone _____ Fax _____ Email _____

From where did you buy this book _____

Ref:GDA-G&G

Detach and mail this form to
SPSS South Asia, #20, 11ᵗʰ A Main, Millers Road,
Vasanth Nagar, Bangalore-560 052
Phone:080-22206625-28; Fax: 080-41858068;
Email: marketing@spss.co.in

*Photocopies will not be entertained